Napa Navigator
A Guide for Mapping Your Wine Country Odyssey

Ralph & Lahni DeAmicis

Cuore Libre Publishing
Napa California

Napa Navigator
A Guide for Mapping Your Wine Country Odyssey
Third Edition
Ralph & Lahni DeAmicis

Published by
Cuore Libre Publishing
Napa, California

To Order Copies Phone visit
www.AmicisTours.com

Copyright © 2013, 2014, 2022, 2023
by Ralph & Lahni DeAmicis
Photos: Lahni DeAmicis
Maps: Ralph DeAmicis
ISBN 978-1-0881-6893-6

Disclaimer: We create these books through extensive research that includes having visited many of these wineries multiple times. But we make no guarantees for the accuracy of the information included herein, and accept no responsibility for any losses or inconvenience you may suffer from using this product. Important: Our advice is intended to help you stay safe while you enjoy the region, but mixing alcohol and driving is a risky endeavor. We suggest that you approach it cautiously by having a designated or professional driver. We want you to have a fun time in Wine Country and come back and visit again and again.

Ralph & Lahni DeAmicis

Contents

Maps Directory 4

Chapter 1: Getting Around Napa 7

Chapter 2: Around the City of Napa 19

Chapter 3: The Heart, Oakville & Rutherford 29

Chapter 4: St. Helena & the Northern Valley 39

Chapter 5: The Canyons & Mountains 53

Chapter 6: The ABC's of Wine Tasting 57

Chapter 7: Winery Directory 59

About the Authors 137

Other Titles 138

Map Directory

The Towns and Main Routes in the North Bay   6

The Main North Bay Viticulture Areas   8

The Main North Bay Viticulture Areas   10

Napa Valley Crossroads   12

A: Los Carneros AVA   14

B: Wineries from Yountville to Saint Helena   16

Hotels & Restaurants Around the City of Napa   18

C: Wineries from Napa City North to Oak Knoll   20

D: Stags Leap AVA   22

E: Oak Knoll & Stags Leap   24

F: From Yountville to Saint Helena   26

G: Oakville & Rutherford, the Valley's Heart   28

Napa American Viticulture Areas (AVA)   30

H: Judgment of Paris Wineries   32

I: More Wineries from Yountville to Saint Helena   34

J: Wineries Around Saint Helena   36

K: Saint Helena to Calistoga   38

L: North of Saint Helena to Larkmead Lane   40

M: Wineries Around Calistoga   42

N: Wineries Close to Calistoga   44

O: Mount Veeder   46

P: Coombsville   48

Q: Soda Canyon & Atlas Peak   50

R: Sage Canyon & Chiles Valley   52

S: Spring Mountain   54

T: Deer Park & Howell Mountain   56

Introduction to the Napa Navigator

This book is written from the perspective of two tour guides, a profession that views the region from two sides. We see our guests' wide-eyed, slightly inebriated enjoyment of the great wines and remarkable experiences, and we also see how much work our winery neighbors put into creating them. It is a synergistic relationship, which is why this region continues to evolve and so have our books. Our intention is to help you enjoy your time in Wine Country so we base our recommendations on our many clients' experiences and comments over the years.

Napa has a history of prosperity that goes back to the time of the native people, whose language had no word for starvation, so abundant was food. When the first westerners arrived the Napa River opened a door to the world that brought the Valley early recognition for its beauty, fertility, and delicious wines. Its broad sun-drenched valley floor, bordered by rocky, forested hills stretches from the cool edges of the bay, north to the warm feet of Mount Saint Helena. It encompasses an amazing variety of growing territories that provide winemakers with a wonderful diversity of grapes and flavors, in a remarkably convenient region that makes it a delight for visitors.

The Towns and Main Routes in the North Bay

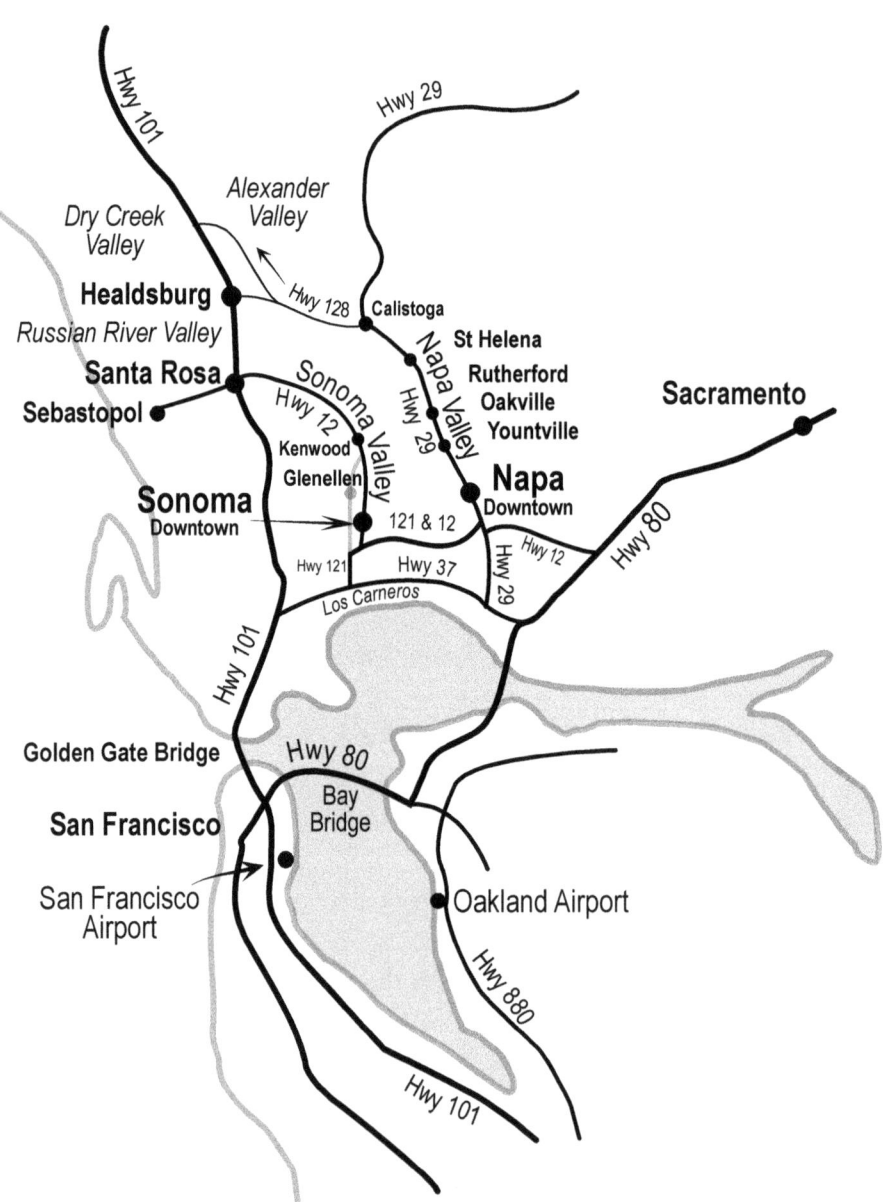

Chapter 1: Getting Around Napa Valley

Napa and Sonoma are the world's two top wine tourism destinations. Napa is a third of the size of Sonoma and significantly warmer and sunnier, allowing them to grow more of the expensive Cabernet Sauvignon, which fills sixty percent of their vineyards. The valley is thirty miles long and, at its widest, five miles across. The valley floor is bordered on both sides by steep hills. At the base of the valley is the San Pablo Bay, with its cool Carneros winds, and nightly fogs, that support Chardonnay and Pinot Noir vineyards. As you go northwest up the valley it gets increasingly warmer.

At the town of Saint Helena, the valley narrows to a mile across. Farther north, it widens and gets even warmer around Calistoga at the foot of an ancient volcano called Mount Saint Helena. Beyondthe distinctive cone are Lake County to the northeast and Sonoma County to the northwest. Napa has been an important tourist destination since the late 1800's, originally for its hots springs and health spas. It is a beautiful place and besides the wineries, of which there are about a thousand, the region has lovely hotels, restaurants, shopping, culinary programs, mud baths, horseback riding and lots of golf courses.

The Main North Bay Viticulture Areas

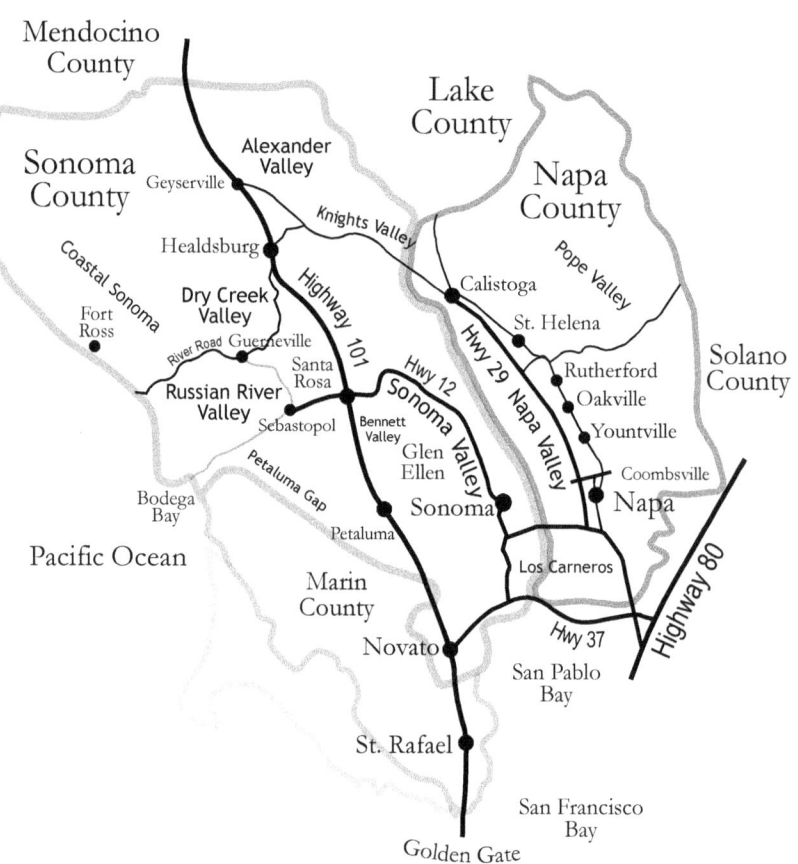

The growing areas are divided into districts called 'American Viticulture Areas' or AVAs. They describe growing regions that produce unique wine characteristics due to their climatic and geologic characters. As of 2020 Napa has sixteen AVA's, ranging from cool Los Carneros at the base of the valley up to hot Calistoga at the top. Some AVAs include the rocky, basaltic Mount Veeder AVA in the southwest, volcanic Howell Mountain AVA in the northeast, the rustic Wild Horse Valley AVA in the southeast and the breezy Spring Mountain AVA in the northwest. The variety of territories placed so close together is remarkable and in the middle of all of them are Oakville and Rutherford, two of the world's most famous wine growing locations and well-known AVAs.

The wide diversity is due to Napa's eclectic geological nature, which is more varied than most growing regions and its numerous climatic zones. That allows the local vintners to grow widely different grapes in a relatively small valley, one fifth the size of Bordeaux. In the south near the bay, Napa grows the grapes of northern France (Burgundy and Champagne), in the center, it grows the grapes of southwest France (Bordeaux and Cahors) and at the peak of the valley, they grow the grapes of Sicily.

Navigation Tip: Watch for the small white on blue winery signs (one foot high by three feet wide) placed at eye level at the side of the road. They are often the only signs that announce the winery before their entrance. They are also sometimes used to mark hotels.

Navigating the Main Roads Easily

Because it is relatively small, getting around Napa is easy. The valley roads are laid out like a ladder. Highway 29 (St Helena Highway) and the Silverado Trail are the ladder's uprights, going from the southeast to the northwest. Between them is the Napa River, which has its sources near Mount Saint Helena, running south the length of the valley through the city of Napa, and emptying into the San Pablo Bay at the city of Vallejo.

The Main Roads of Southern Sonoma & Napa

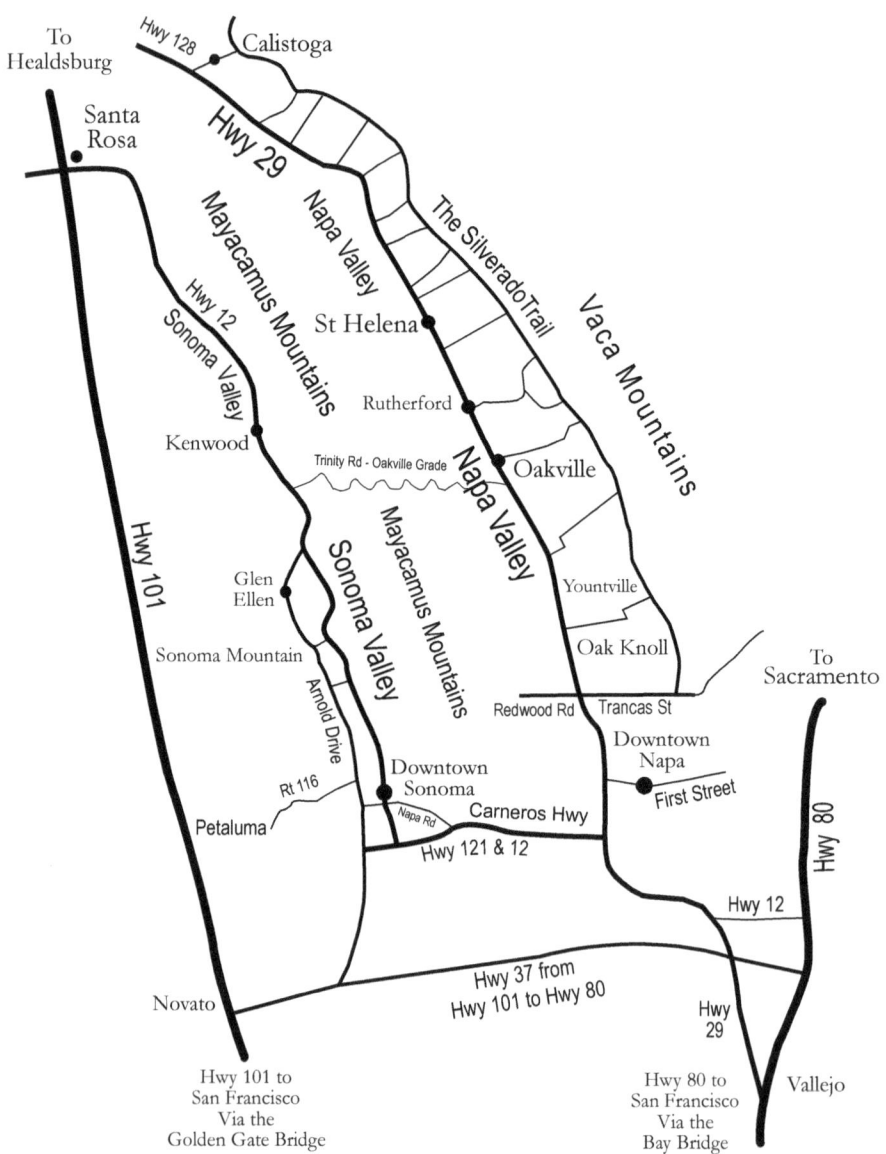

Highway 29 is the 'main road' that connects the downtowns and has a few different names along its route. It parallels the tracks of the Wine Train, a tourist attraction that uses a right-of-way established in the late 1800's, to bring tourists to Sam Brannan's Calistoga Hot Springs. The Silverado Trail began as the Wappo tribe's trading trail that wound through the eastern hills to avoid the flooded valley floor during the winter rainy season.

These two 'upright' roads are connected, east to west, about every mile, by bridges and crossroads that form the 'rungs' of the ladder. Heading north, these roads begin with Trancas Street, which is the northern commercial edge of the city of Napa. The next three are Yountville Cross Road, Oakville Cross Road and Rutherford Road which are each named for their towns. Note: Rutherford starts at Hwy 29 and then splits into Conn Creek Road and Skellenger Lane with both making the final connections to the Silverado Trail.

Next are the crossroads for the town of Saint Helena; Zinfandel Lane, Pope Street, Pratt Avenue, Deer Park Road, (which continues up the hill to Howell Mountain and the town of Angwin) Lodi Lane and Bale Lane. In the northernmost part of the valley the crossroads of the town of Calistoga are Larkmead Lane, Dunaweal Lane, Lincoln Avenue and Tubbs Lane. The latter was named for the founder of the winery that is now Chateau Montelena, Alfred Tubbs. Both Chateau Montelena and Calistoga's Old Faithful Geyser are located on Tubbs Lane and from the Silverado Trail end it meets the route that begins a steep climb up Mount Saint Helena into Lake County. From the other end, you can connect to the road the brings you north, over the hills, into Sonoma's popular Alexander Valley.

While Highway 29 is home to most of the oldest wineries, many very interesting wineries make their homes on the crossroads and the 'Trail'. For example, you'll find Cliff Lede on Yountville Cross Road, Silver Oak, Groth, B Cellars and Plumpjack are all on Oakville Cross Road. Caymus, Frog's Leap, and Round

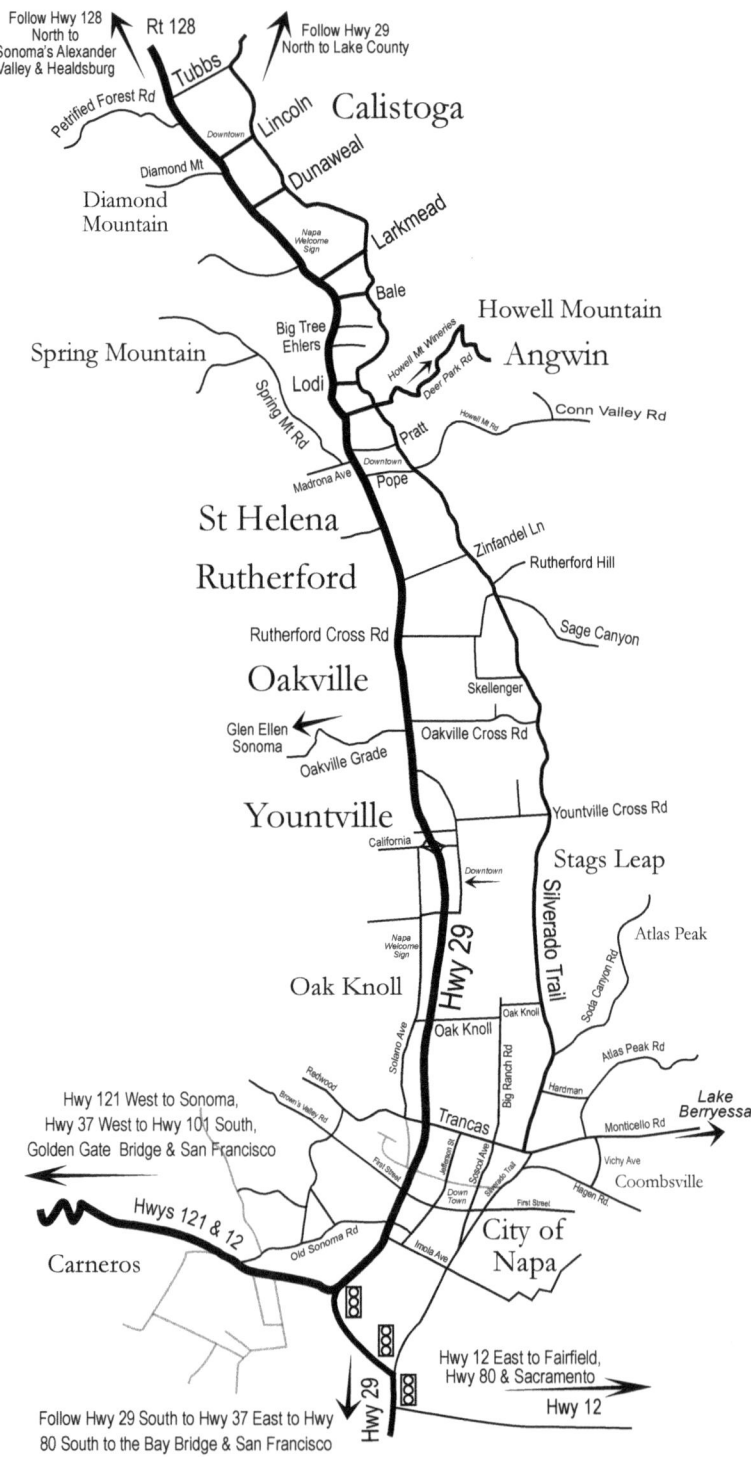

Pound arhe on Rutherford Road or the connecting Conn Creek Road, and Kelham Family is on Zinfandel Lane. North of Saint Helena, Duckhorn is at the corner of Silverado and Lodi Lane, notably the shortest crossroad. In Northern Napa, many of the biggest wineries are on the crossroads; Frank Family and Larkmead Vineyards are on Larkmead Lane (the former Family Estate of Lillie Coit, as in Coit Tower in San Francisco. Sterling (famous for its tramway), Clo Pegase and Girard are all on Dunaweal Lane, while Chateau Montelena, and Tamber Bey are on Tubbs Lane, which is the furthest north crossroad that connects Highway 29 to the Silverado Trail.

A perfect example of the Silverado Trail's importance is the Stags Leap AVA in the southeast corner of the valley. The Trail, along a short stretch of road, bisects about twenty well known and, in some cases, prestigious wineries including Shafer, Stag's Leap Cellars, Silverado Vineyards, Chimney Rock, Pine Ridge, Realm and Quixote. **Warning:** Some roads don't cross between Hwy 29 and the Silverado Trail, so check the maps. The great thing about this road arrangement is that it makes it possible to travel from winery to winery by only making right turns which is both safer and faster on busy days. This is helpful in a place where people routinely drink alcohol and get behind the wheel.

Clusters of Wineries

The oldest wineries were located along Highway 29, giving them easy access to the main road and the train tracks for moving wagons full of grapes and wine. The oldest stone wineries like Far Niente, Inglenook, Beringer and Christian Brothers, now the CIA Saint Helena campus, were built into small hillsides. This served their gravity-fed design which sent the grape wagons up the slope to the powerfully built second floor where the grapes were unloaded into the fermentation tanks. When the wine was ready to go into the aging barrels, a valve was opened and gravity carried the juice through a hose to the barrels on the floor below, where they were rolled into the adjacent cave.

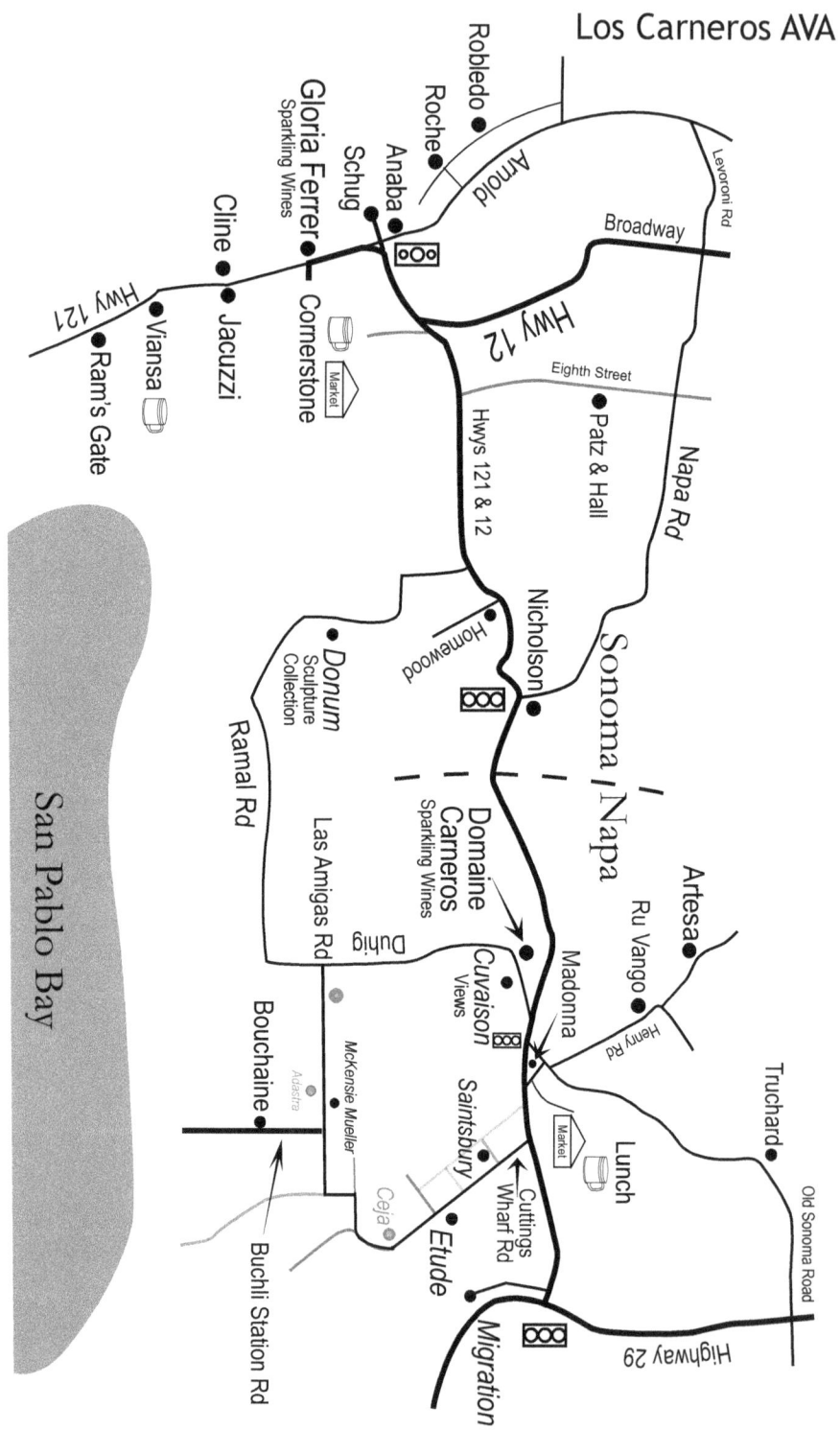

As you drive north on Highway 29 there are areas where the vineyards sit edge to edge. In the 1960's and 70's, when there were only about twenty wineries, the most popular were on the north bound side of the narrow road to better catch customers coming up from the towns around the bay. Tastings were free and visitors would go into the wineries on the right side of the road all the way to Charles Krug, just north of Saint Helena. Then they would cross the street and visit Christian Brothers for one more tasting before heading home. This was a great strategy on a narrow road with questionable shoulders and lots of drunks.

This brings us to a story. The modern Robert Mondavi Winery was started in the 1960's and it is on the south bound, left side of the road. Mondavi's new winery would be among the first visitors would see, which could be great for business if he could convince people to stop on their way up valley. By the time they were heading south they already had enough wine in them. Even though there was available land on the north bound side of the road, he wanted the renowned To Kalon vineyard, on the south bound side.

He was aiming to make world class wines, and this western slope is where many of Napa's historically important Oakville and Rutherford vineyards are found. It is well drained, rocky bench land that is shaded in the late afternoon by Mount St. John, protecting the vines from the punishing western sunshine. But, what's best for the grapes wasn't as good for getting customers in the door, so Bob Mondavi used some innovative 'tricks' to get people into his new winery and onto his tours.

Then as now, on weekend mornings traffic north on Highway 29 can be heavy. He would have his son Michael drive his car up from downtown Napa and then sit in the road with this turn signal on, while cars stacked up behind him. Someone, maybe Bob, would be holding up a sign that said, 'Free Tours and Wine' and waving people in. When Michael relented and made the turn,

Wineries from Yountville to Saint Helena

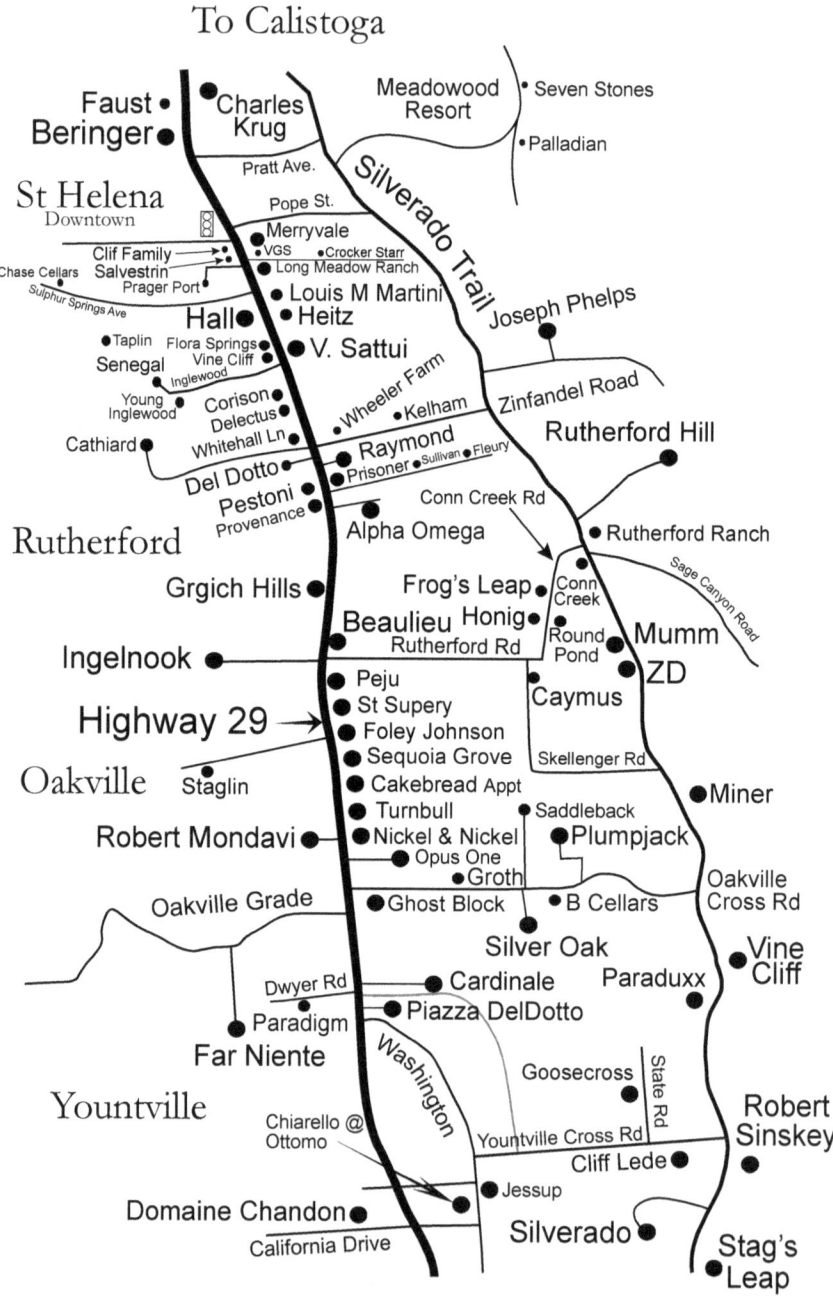

some cars would typically follow him. He would park, jump out of the car and walk the visitors into the tasting room. Then he would head downtown again.

There is more traffic on Hwy 29 than ever before, and the town of Saint Helena is a north-bound bottleneck. If you are going up valley past the town, bypass the congestion by taking the Silverado Trail north. It is often clear sailing from Trancas Street, all the way to Calistoga. If you are going up Hwy 29 and want to miss the bottleneck, Zinfandel Lane is the last crossroad you can take over to the Silverado Trail. At the end of the day southbound traffic backs up in Rutherford and Oakville, more often on Highway 29, but less often on the Trail. There is a wonderful group of wineries on the Silverado Trail in the south part of valley in the Oak Knoll and Stags Leap districts, but north of Yountville Cross Road the Trail wineries are spread out.

Hotels & Restaurants Around the City of Napa

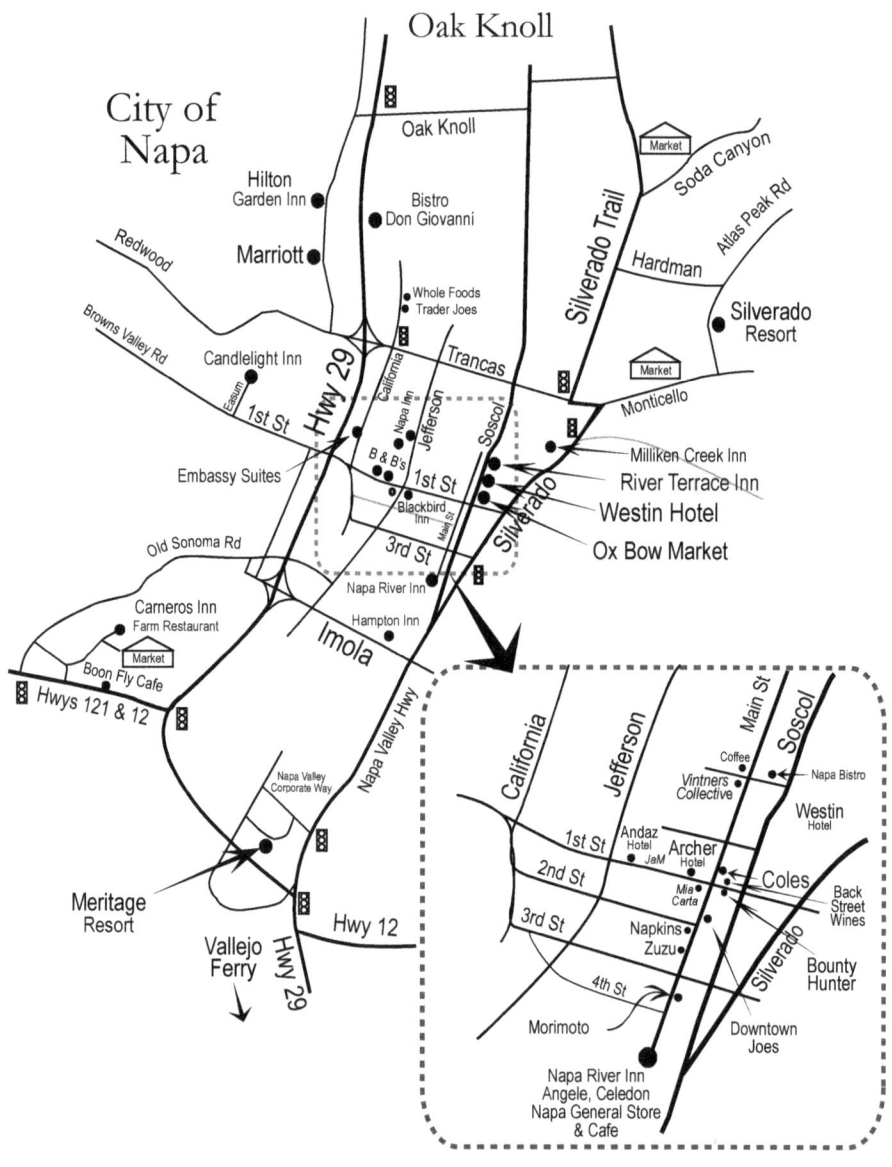

Chapter 2: Around the City of Napa

Downtown Napa sits on the valley floor where the Napa River meets Napa Creek, just south of the oxbow bend in the river, that made navigation any farther north impractical for sailing ships. It was the site of the native tribe's permanent camp called, not surprisingly, Napa. Because the Napa River is navigable, this area has always had a commercial advantage compared to downtown Sonoma, which was established as a Spanish military camp, far from the bayside docks. During the Spanish and Mexican period, shipping was dominated by Americans from New England and the Pacific Northwest. Those American ship Captains became Napa's first major investors. As of 2020, there are about forty tasting rooms in downtown storefronts plus more wineries in the corporate parks. We don't list those downtown tasting rooms because, unlike wineries that are tied to vineyards and wine making facilities, store fronts come and go. You can find lists of the downtown tasting rooms, which are fun to visit with less risk of a DUI, at the Visitor's Centers and hotels.

Looking West from the City of Napa to Mount Veeder

To the west of downtown Napa is Mount Veeder, the only basaltic mountain vineyards in this otherwise volcanic region.

Wineries from Napa City North to Oak Knoll

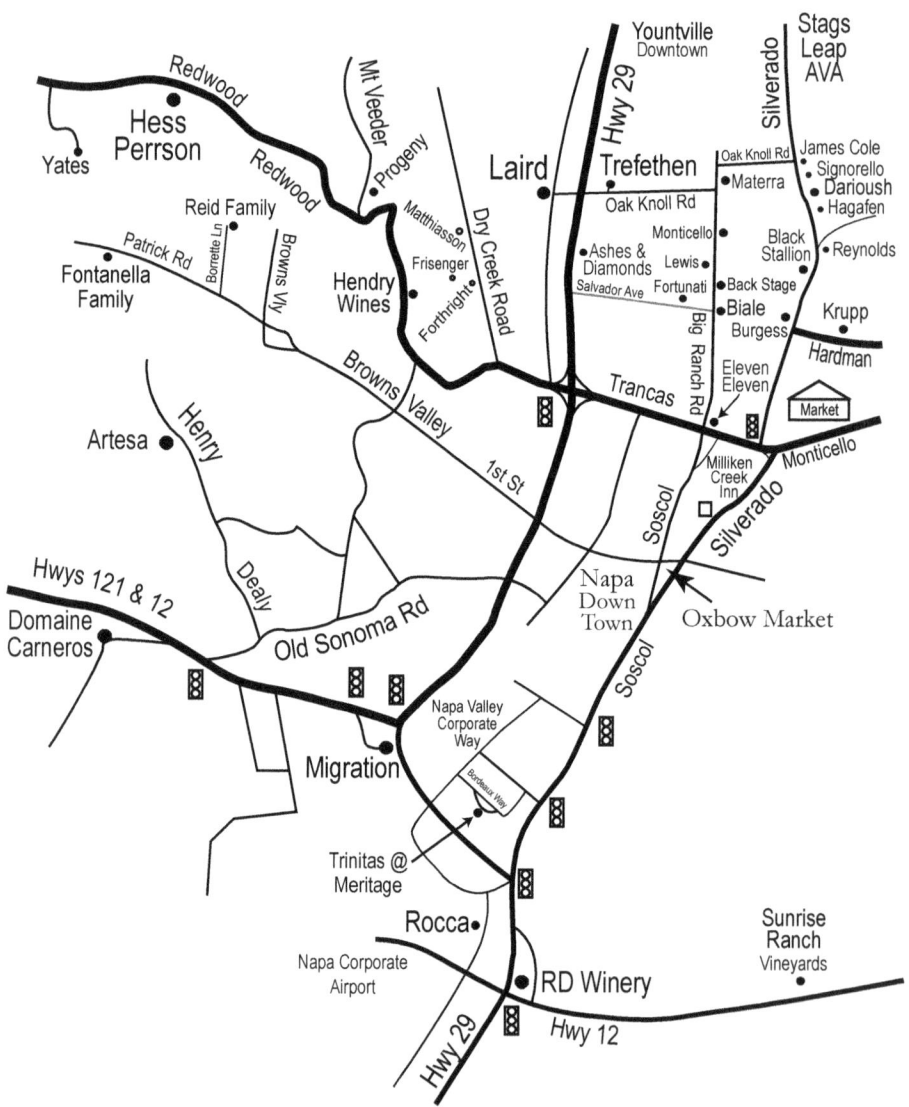

This alkaline rock produces softer wines profiles including among the Cabernets, an especially nice quality in such a highly structured wine. Veeder's rugged hills and narrow, winding roads have never supported easy winery visits. Both fires and floods have closed the roads for weeks at a time. There are some wonderful family wineries hidden up there including long time grower Hendry and relatively new on the scene, Fontanella, but the big winery destination there is The Hess Collection, a large winery with a diverse line of wines and a world class modern art collection. It is housed in two stone barns, built at the beginning of the Twentieth Century.

Looking East from the City of Napa to Coombsville

This up-and-coming AVA is filled with beautiful, rolling hills that become heavily wooded ridges in the east. They are dotted with newer premium and ultra-premium, by-appointment wineries. There was no history of BIG wineries in Coombsville, because it's too cool and not at all flat, so it was long considered marginal for vineyards, but useful for grazing. But then, intrepid growers using their own weather stations, found locations on Coombsville's hillsides that are hospitable to numerous varietals including Cabernet.

On your way to the wineries, you'll still see livestock and the pretty Shadybrook Winery incorporates both worlds by having horse stables on their shared property that offers trail rides. Visiting Coombsville takes planning and a good map but it's lovely and convenient. Thanks to the hillside locations, the wineries are small and may feature cave tastings including wineries like Caldwell, Palmaz and Solano.

Immediately North of the City Napa

The northern border of the City of Napa is Trancas Street, a four-lane local road where you'll find the chain stores and coffee shops that don't exist up in the protected valley. Just north of

Stags Leap AVA

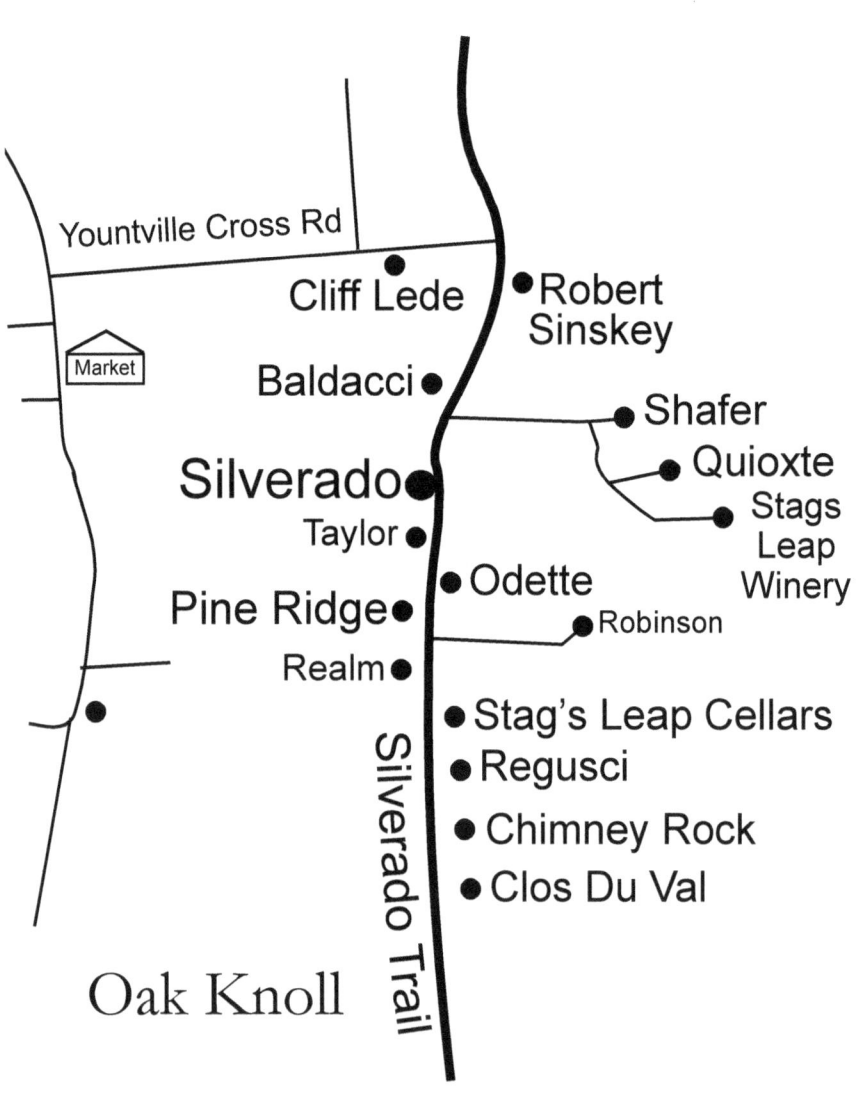

Trancas Street is the Oak Knoll AVA, a magical place for grapes because of the wide variety that can thrive here. Some standouts here are Trefethen (built in the 1800's) and Darioush, both known for their architecture, and Del Dotto (Atlas Peak), with its wonderful barrel tasting in their historic cave. Other popular wineries include; Andretti (as in Mario, the race car driver), Biale (known for their Zinfandels), Monticello (including a small scale replica of the Jefferson home), Laird (the building is a verdigris copper pyramid), Elyse (unusual varietals), Bell (secluded but convenient), Luna (luscious), Signorello (brand-new, rebuilt winery), James Cole (very personalized experience), Black Stallion (fun, social experience), Hagafen (the Hebrew word for wine, producing excellent kosher wines), Reynolds (family owned), Eleven Eleven (interesting wines right off Trancas Street), William Hill (expansive vineyard views) and Ashes and Diamonds (modern Millennial favorite).

Just north of Oak Knoll, on the Silverado Trail, is the spectacular Stags Leap District, a favorite of Cabernet aficionados worldwide. The rugged topography, heavy overnight fog, volcanic soils and strong afternoon sunlight produce very bright wines, possessing profound depth. Located in the valley's southeastern corner, it's convenient even for San Francisco based visitors.

Every winery here is good and they include Clo du Val (Cabs plus Pinots), Chimney Rock (South African Dutch architecture), Regusci Family (architecture, history and views from the patio), Stag's Leap Cellars (of the "Judgment of Paris" wine competition fame), Shafer (seriously elegant), Quixote (architectural destination), Stags' Leap Winery (Petite Syrah and history), Pine Ridge (pretty with a great cave), Odette (a very modern, Millennial style part of the Plumpjack group of wineries), Silverado Vineyards (Disney family owned with great views and tasty, reasonably priced wines), Baldacci (brand new caves and hospitality center), Robert Sinskey (gardens, herbs, food pairings plus Pinots), Cliff Lede (very romantic) and just north of the AVA line, the totally fun and scenic Goosecross.

Oak Knoll & Stags Leap

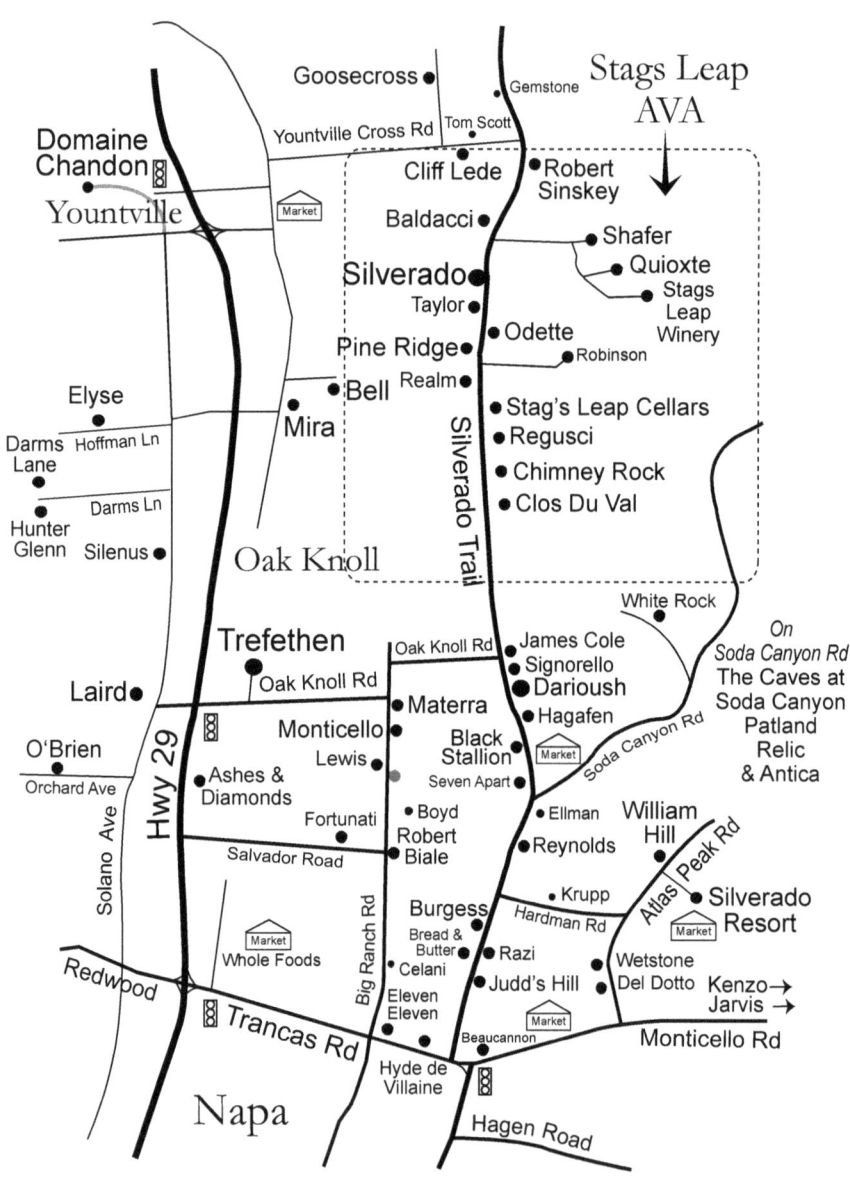

The northern border of the Stags Leap AVA is 'Yountville Cross Road' and that's a quick, scenic way to go from the Silverado Trail to Highway 29. The little town of Yountville is the "foodie capital" of wine country and it's grown up in the past fifty years from a little farming village that was also home to a bevy of cheap bars to serve the Veteran's housed across the road. It's frugal solitude also made it popular with the Bay Area bikers. The bars and bikers are gone, replaced with a stunning number of world class eateries and excellent tasting rooms. The most notable Yountville winery is just across Highway 29 from the downtown, in its own expansive grounds, the festive and busy, Domaine Chandon. This was the first important European winery to invest here in 1970 and they are famous for their sparkling wines. They led the charge that resulted in downtown Yountville becoming a destination, filled with tasting rooms, restaurants, stores and hotels.

Just outside town are several notable wineries that you can visit. Cliff Lede on Yountville Cross Road (look for the Canadian flag) is a lovely, small winery that does both bar (walk-in) and seated (appointment) tastings in the garden. Across the way on State Lane is the long-time favorite Goosecross, small, fun with great outdoor seating next to the vines. Just north of the crossroad on Silverado is the popular Paraduxx with their food pairings in the garden.

Just north of Yountville on Highway 29 are a string of wineries; the impressive Piazza Del Dotto (the family's third winery), with their expansive patios, busy bars and caves, Cosentino (serendipitously good), casual Napa Cellars and Folie a Deux share a location and the remote, serious collector winery, Cardinale, in their imposing stone building perched on a knoll on the right (east) side of the road.

Across the way to the west, sitting in the middle of their vineyard is the prestigious Far Niente. This was built in the 1800's and they are among the top echelon of producers, sitting here in

From Yountville to Saint Helena

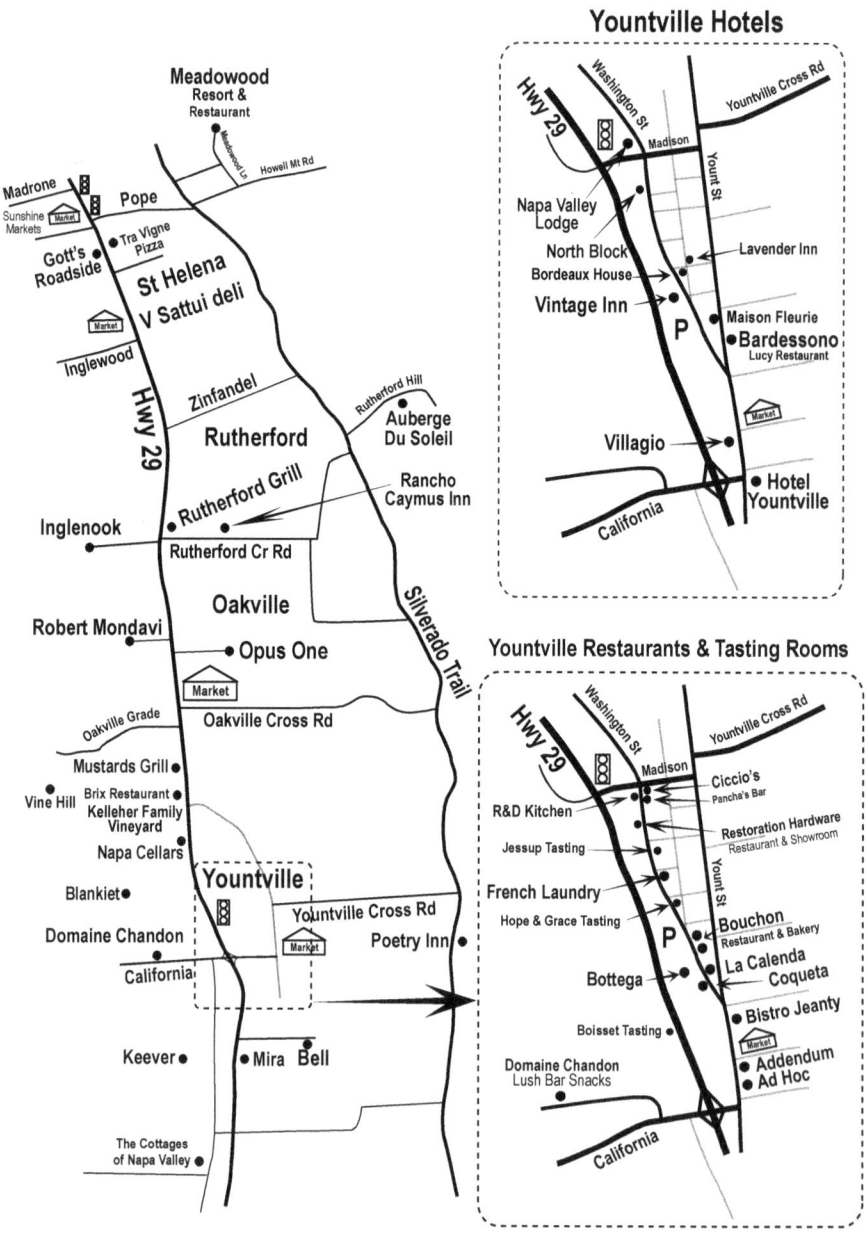

the heart of Oakville. A little side note: above Far Niente, on the top of the mountain ridge, are two mansions with a small house in between. That was once the long-time home of Robin Williams, the wonderful actor and comedian. He had a challenge with alcoholism and did his rehab at the hospital in Saint Helena. He later quipped, "I did my rehab in wine country to keep my options open".

Oakville & Rutherford, the Valley's Heart

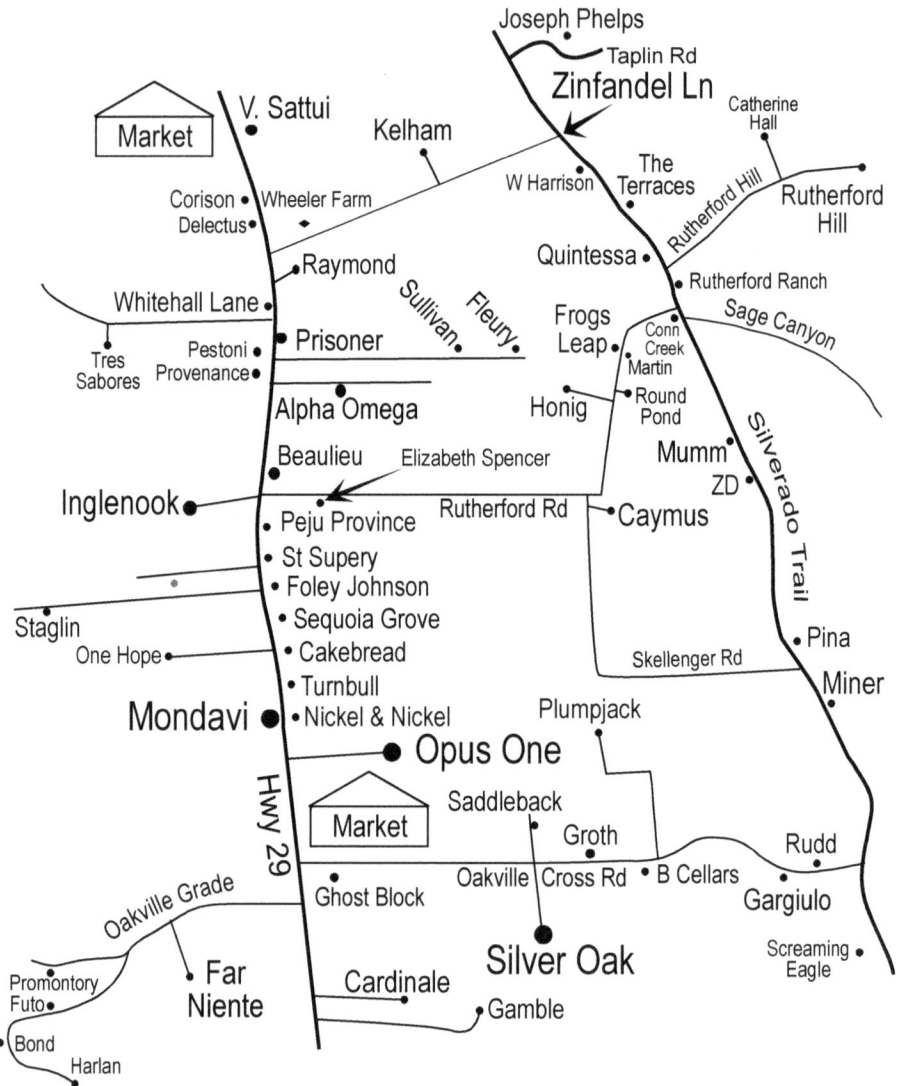

Chapter 3: The Heart, Oakville & Rutherford

Since grape growing began in Napa, farmers preferred this level and wide stretch of sun-drenched land, where you can drive a tractor a long way before turning around. The well-drained volcanic benchlands along the edge help Cabernet thrive, while the ancient riverbeds in the center favor Merlot. The valley's cool overnight fogs withdraw early enough that the grapes enjoy the color rich morning sunlight. Then, Mount Saint John shades the grapes in the late afternoon from the hot, bleaching western sun. For growing Napa's favorite red grapes, it doesn't get easier than this. *See the map on page 190.*

Geologically, Oakville and Rutherford are different. Both are influenced by volcanic ridges that border the valley, but Rutherford's vines are flavored by iron rich minerals, locally called 'Rutherford dust', the source of which is a red mountain in the eastern hills. This distinctive red soil was fanned across the district over millennia by streams. It makes the wines both softer and deeper, compared to the more muscular Oakville vines.

Driving North on Highway 29, after Yountville, is the 'Welcome to Napa' sign. Behind it, surrounded by vineyards, is the extraordinary Far Niente Winery, built in the late 1800's. On

Napa American Viticulture Areas (AVA)

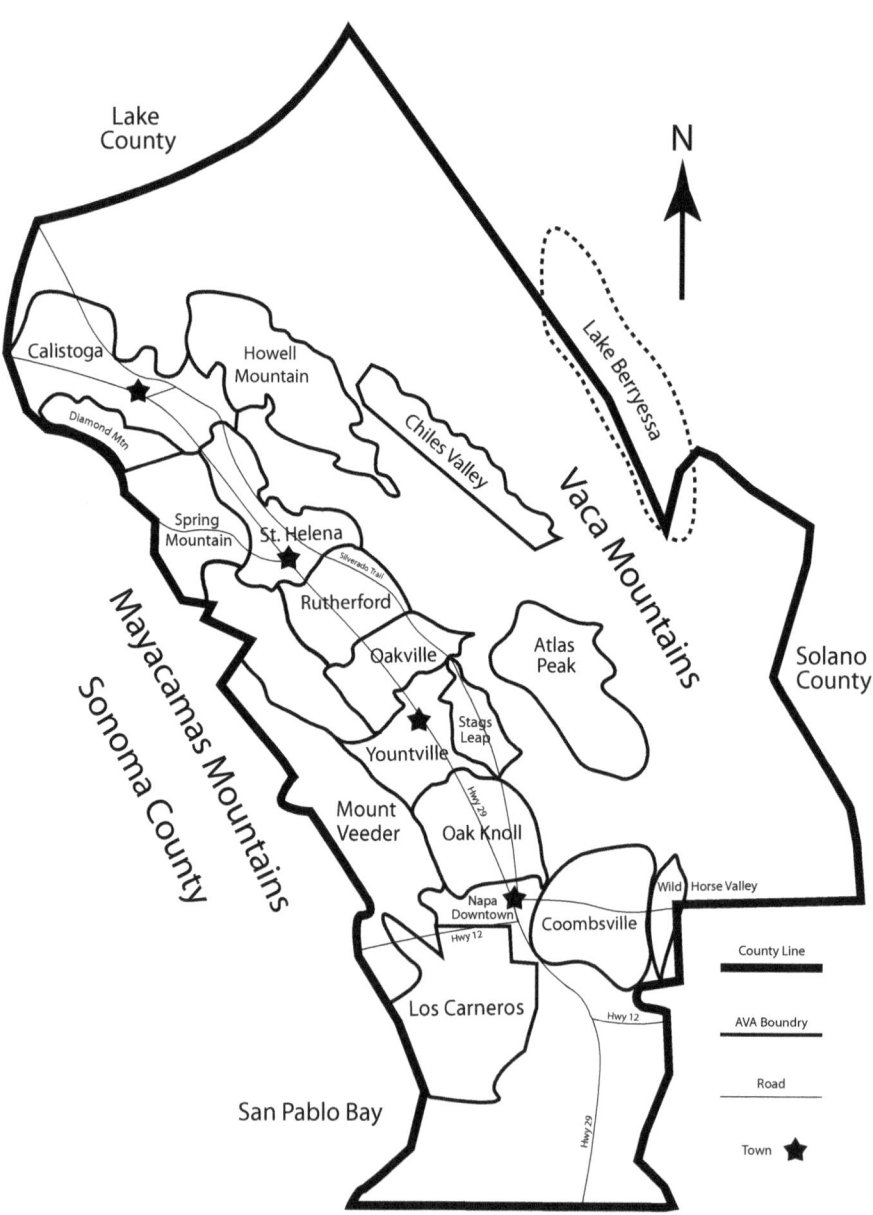

the hills above it are the vines of the ultra-premium Harlan and Promontory Wineries, and above those is the former estate of the actor, Robin Williams. Across the road is the ultra-premium Cardinale Winery. This gives you an idea of the neighborhood you are driving into.

The diminutive Oakville Grocery, a popular breakfast and lunch stop, is California's oldest continuously operating market, built in 1881. Next door is their Museum and Wine Merchant. Hint: Pick up your lunch before 11:00am and return later to use their picnic tables, to avoid waiting in the long lines.

Starting at the grocery is a string of premium wineries, one after another; Opus One, Napa's first expense account wine, the expansive Robert Mondavi Winery, Nickel and Nickel, making single varietal wines, Turnbull with its gallery, the ever popular Cakebread, eclectic Foley Johnson, charming Sequoia, elegant St. Supéry, festive Peju and tiny Elizabeth Spencer in the old Rutherford post office.

Next are the historic wineries. Inglenook was Napa's first grand estate, currently the home of Francis Ford and Eleanor Coppola. Built in the 1800's by Captain Niebaum, one of California's wealthiest men and designed by Hamden McIntyre, the engineer behind many of Napa's historic wineries, it is one of the valley's loveliest properties. The Coppolas began buying pieces of the broken-up estate in the 70's, with movie profits, and eventually reassembled the original property.
Beaulieu Vineyards (meaning beautiful view and abbreviated as BV) was founded in 1904 and survived Prohibition by producing church wine. It has regular and reserve tasting rooms and a statue of André Tchelistcheff, their Russian-born winemaker from 1938 to 1972, who was extremely influential in early Napa. Oakville Cross Road is home to classic Groth, popular Silver Oak, rustic Saddleback, newer but gracious B Cellars, small but mighty Plumpjack and two more ultra-premium wineries, elegant Rudd and cloistered, but charming, Gargiulo. Here is an

Judgment of Paris Wineries

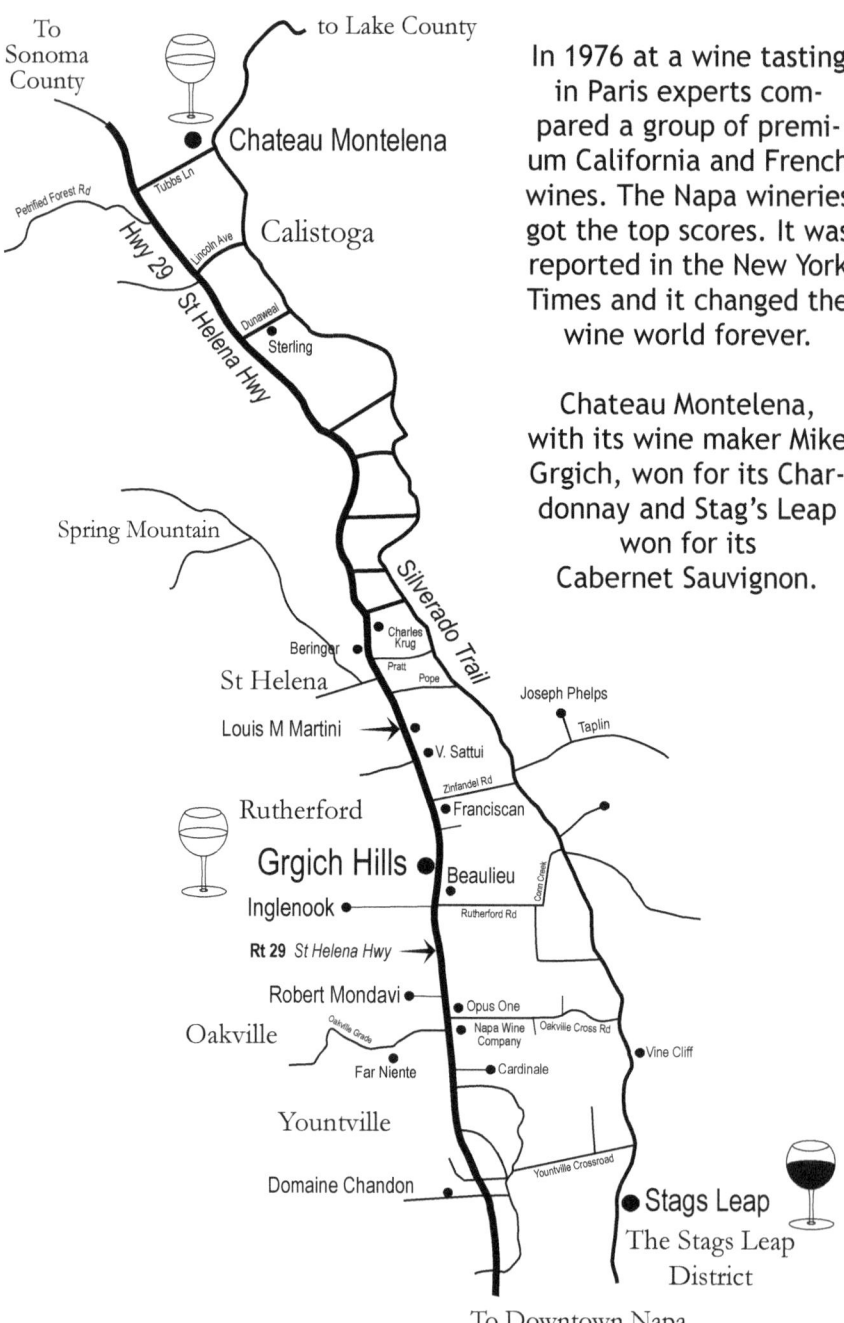

In 1976 at a wine tasting in Paris experts compared a group of premium California and French wines. The Napa wineries got the top scores. It was reported in the New York Times and it changed the wine world forever.

Chateau Montelena, with its wine maker Mike Grgich, won for its Chardonnay and Stag's Leap won for its Cabernet Sauvignon.

interesting wine geek point: on Silverado Trail, south of the intersection and below the road are the vineyards of the ultra-premium, ridiculously expensive Screaming Eagle. Across the road, the hillside vineyards are used by the stellar Joseph Phelps Winery to make some of their most expensive wines. Another sign that, grape wise, this is a fancy neighborhood!

Farther north on the Silverado Trail are two outliers; Miner Family Winery built into the hillside, with their approachable wines and great views, and Mumm Napa, the French based sparkling wine label. In both cases, their vineyards are far away, so calling them Rutherford wineries is a misnomer, but they are both fun and Mumm has a fantastic photography museum. Two notable wineries nearby are a little one called Piña Napa Valley and organic ZD Wines, with their great views.

At the complicated and dangerous intersection of the Silverado Trail, Sage Canyon Road and Conn Creek Road are four wineries, Conn Creek Winery, with their excellent wine blending seminar, hidden away Rutherford Ranch Winery, ultra-premium Quintessa with its arching stone wall and excellent walking tour and Rutherford Hill, with their paid picnic grounds and views. Rutherford Hill Winery sits at the top of Rutherford Road, past Auberge du Soleil, a restaurant and hotel. Driving west on Conn Creek Road towards Rutherford Road brings you to two popular premium wineries, organic Frog's Leap Winery and the popular Caymus Vineyards.

Farther north on the Silverado Trail are three unique wineries, traditional William Harrison Winery, the gated winery called The Terraces, where the vineyards are planted on steep terraced hillsides, and then above Zinfandel Lane, narrow Taplin Road brings you to the iconic Joseph Phelps Winery, the valley's first winery to produce a Bordeaux-style Cabernet blend. Their vineyards spread around their gracious hospitality center with great views and seating areas.

More Wineries from Yountville to Saint Helena

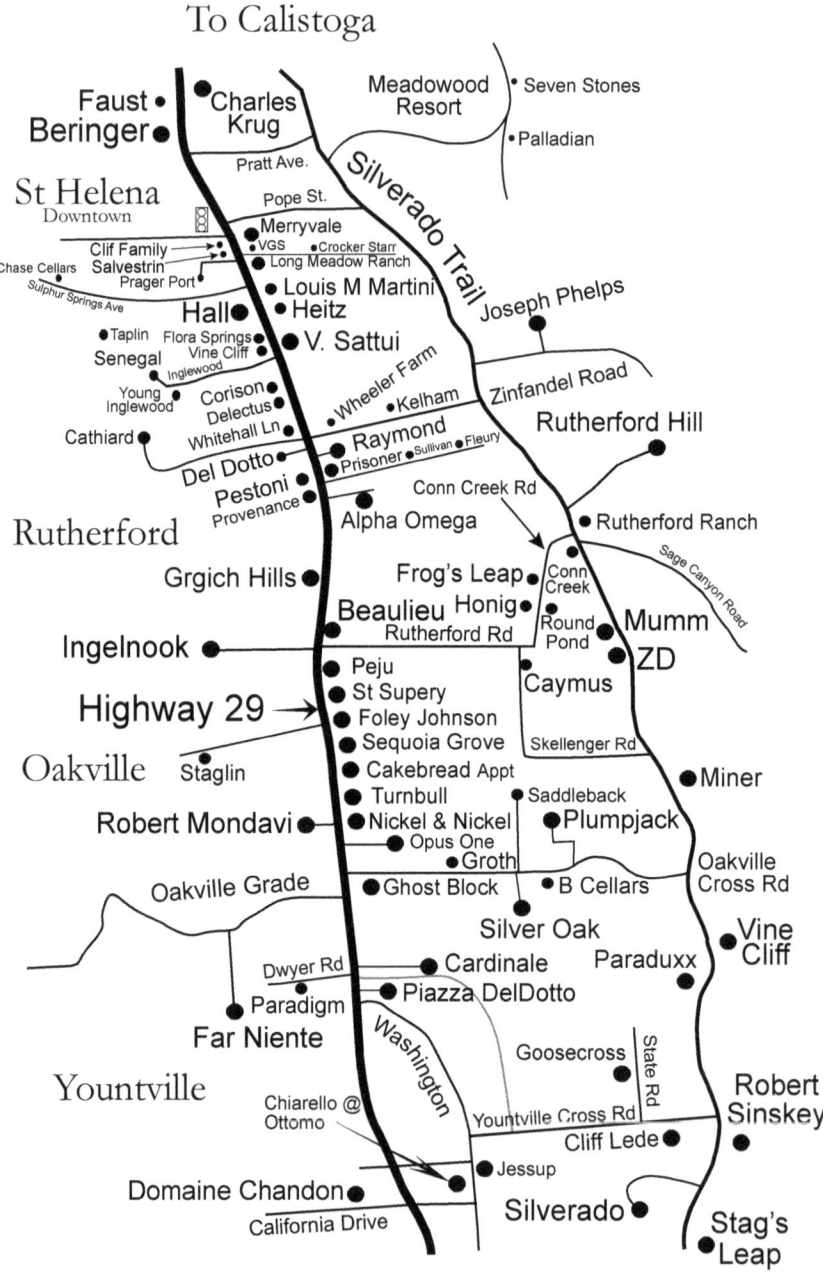

Zinfandel Lane is home to three wineries you can visit. The first two, Kelham Vineyards and Wheeler Farms, are ultra-premiums and behind gates. The third is Raymond Vineyards, but their entrance is due to be moved to Hwy 29.

Head North on Highway 29 from Rutherford to Downtown Saint Helena. This stretch of road has sprouted wineries in the middle-premium range; countrified classic Grgich Hills Estate, started in 1977, the big red producer, Provenance Vineyards, Alpha Omega Winery with their popular patio, Pestoni Family Winery, an old timer started in the 1800's, sleek Whitehall Lane Winery, and tucked behind them is the charmingly rustic Tres Sabores. The Mission style Franciscan Winery was transformed into the monolithic, black painted and chained The Prisoner Wine Co. Down the road behind them are Sullivan Rutherford Estate and quirky Fleury Estate Wines.

The intersection of Highway 29 and Zinfandel Lane gets you to two destination wineries. With their entrance flanked by two giant amphorae, the Del Dotto Estate Winery & Caves is a modern Venetian-style cave winery. This is one of three Del Dotto properties. Raymond Winery is a phantasmagorical exploration of what tasting rooms can be, owned by Jean-Charles Boisset. It is entertaining and educational with a Biodynamic garden that explains this remarkable approach to agriculture. Delectus Winery and Corison Winery are located north of Zinfandel Lane and are favorites of the San Francisco Chronicle wine writers.

The V. Sattui Winery, thanks to its deli, picnic tables and affordable wine, is probably the world's most visited. The Flora Springs Tasting Room, that shares a parking lot with a market and restaurant, also has an historic winery you can visit, that sits behind it at the foot of the hills.

The next landmark is Hall Wines St Helena's silver "Bunny Foo Foo" sculpture, part of their art collection that is spread around their modern winery. Their ultra-premium sister property,

Wineries Around Saint Helena

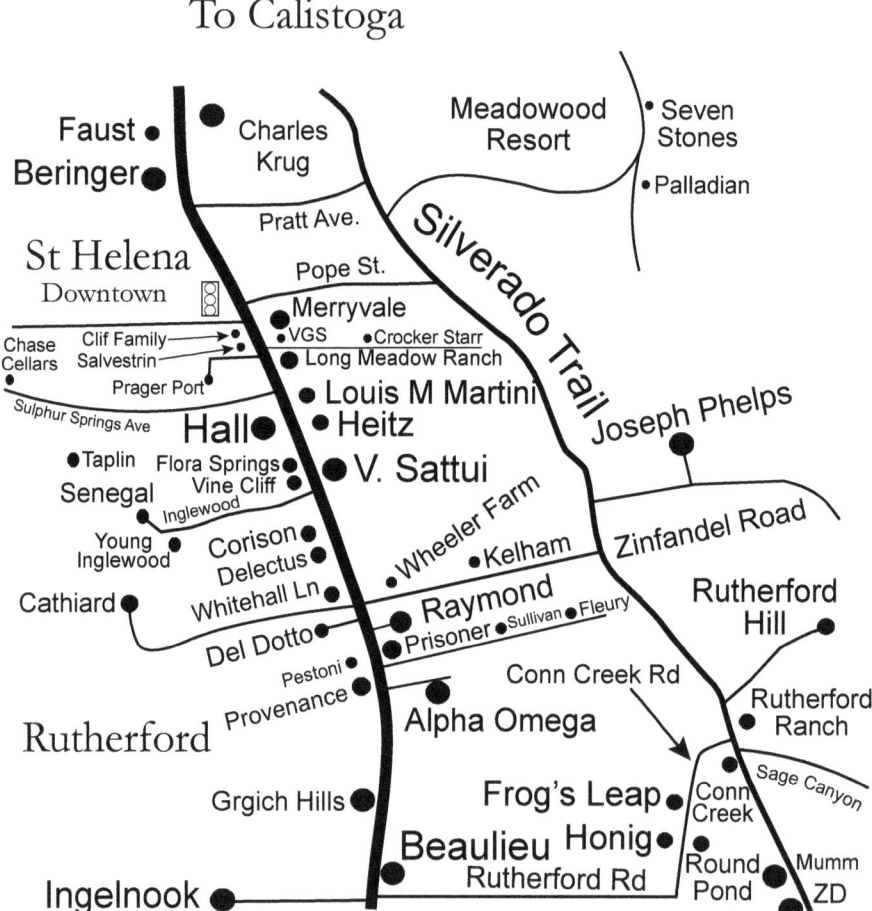

Kathryn Hall Winery (Rutherford), has a unique cave tasting. The cozy Heitz Cellars' tasting room was recently renovated. The well-known Sutter Home Winery is among Napa's most moderately priced, locally produced wines, because the grapes are grown elsewhere. Tucked behind them is the tiny, busy, eccentric Prager Port Works. The grand Louis M. Martini Winery was elegantly transformed by the Gallo family to include bars, comfortable seating areas and a wonderful tasting garden.

Saint Helena to Calistoga

Chapter 4: St. Helena & the Northern Valley

The town of Saint Helena is cool, figuratively and literally. The valley narrows there to only a mile wide, so it enjoys cool shade for much of the day. Across the western hills, the Russian River Valley brings cool ocean breezes and fog that flow over those hills, making life a bit more pleasant in the summertime. Saint Helena was always the fashionable, cosmopolitan up-valley town, where the international winemakers, often former sea captains, lived. The storefronts date from the late 1800's, built by the same masons who constructed the stone wineries. The town resists tearing down those buildings to create new hotels, so there are few nearby places to stay. They make up for that lack with a wonderful variety of restaurants, coffee shops, a fantastic chocolatier, shopping and galleries as well as a reasonably priced local's food market.

As you approach the downtown from the south there are some notable wineries. A diminutive winery called Salvestrin Winery was founded in the 1930's. The VGS Chateau Potelle Winery's tasting room is like a jewel box and their French owner/winemaker produces wonderfully drinkable wines. Nearby is the excellent Crocker and Starr Wines. Davies Vineyards is the still-wine facility of the iconic sparkling house, Schramsberg

North of Saint Helena to Larkmead Lane

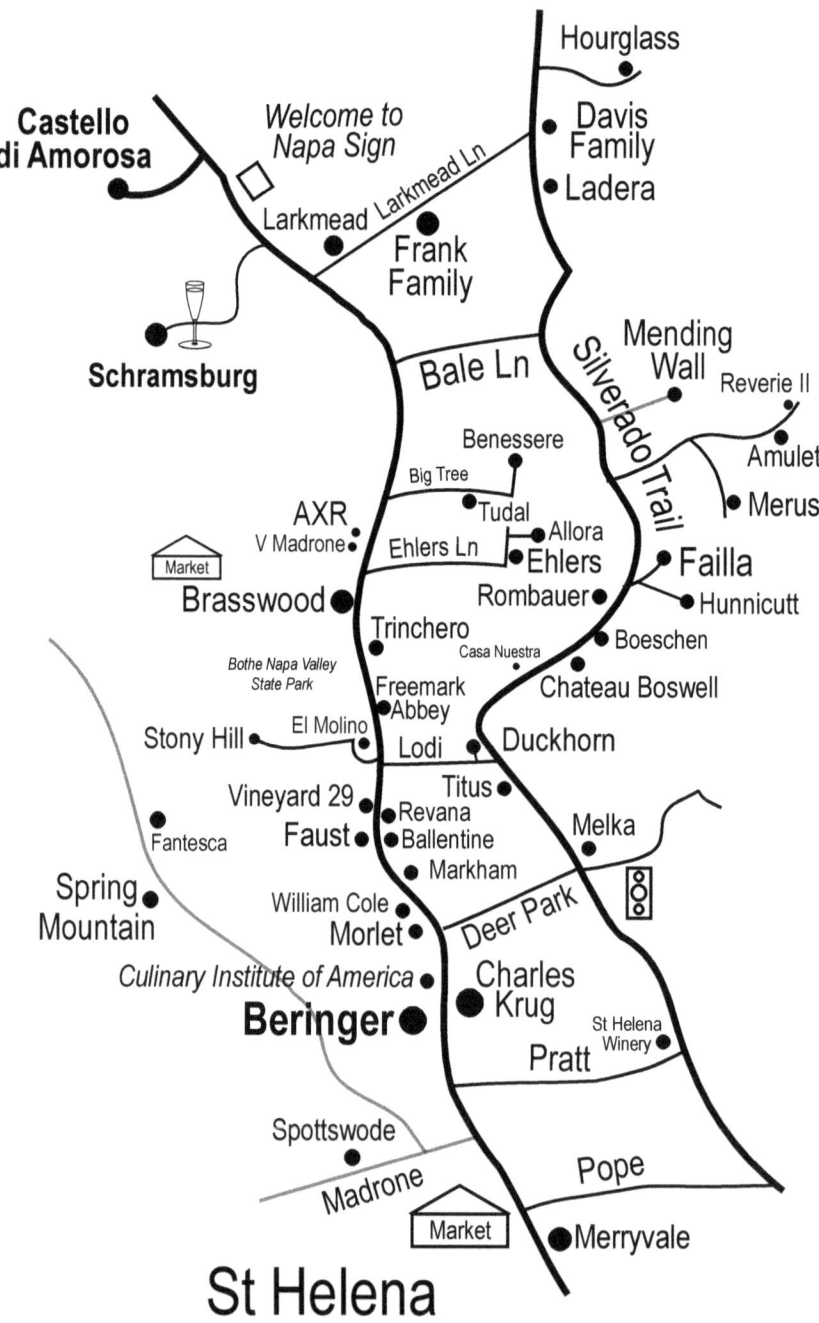

Vineyards. The fun, sport themed Clif Family Winery's tasting room is filled with bicycles and as you may surmise from the name, every kind of Clif Bar you can imagine. You can even enjoy a quick lunch from their Bruschetteria Food Truck on their property.

Another food & wine venue, Long Meadow Ranch's tasting room and their Farmstead Restaurant makes a great visit. Merryvale Vineyards is a fun, downtown, working winery, complete with a giant barrel-room event space and tasting bar. Across the street is the ever-popular Gott's Roadside eatery. On the north side of town, you will find the charming Spottswoode and the small, low-key albeit historic David Fulton Winery. On the Silverado Trail, north of Taplin Road, is the AuburnJames Winery, a premium producer on a pretty property. There are, of course, numerous downtown tasting rooms.

As you leave town and head north, Beringer Vineyards, started in 1876, is immediately on the left. The old stone gate was made for narrow grape wagons, not SUVs, so take it slow. They offer numerous tours and experiences on their expansive property. The grand Rhine House is where they pour the reserve wines, while the regular list is poured in the old winery.

A bit farther in is the Culinary Institute of America (CIA) building that once housed the Christian Brothers Winery. It towers over the road on the left side while the Charles Krug Winery, Napa's oldest winery, hides behind the trees on the right side. Peter Mondavi's family operates CK and the front half of their old winery building is a wonderful tasting salon with an Italian deli and an expansive tasting garden under the trees.

Most tourists only get as far north as downtown Saint Helena because the valley narrows dramatically, slowing down traffic and discouraging all but the brave. To attract visitors to wander farther north, it helps if a winery is extraordinary and northern Napa has several destination wineries.

Wineries Around Calistoga

They include Sterling Vineyards, featuring a tramway that takes you to the top of the hill to enjoy the views with the wines, Schramsberg Vineyards, the maker of sparkling wines in the valley's oldest hillside caves that you will visit during their fascinating tour, the massive Castello di Amorosa, patterned on a Medieval Tuscan castle winery, complete with sheep, and Chateau Montelena Winery, built in the 1800's and famous for being a winner at the Judgment of Paris wine competition in 1976 which put Napa on the international wine map.

North of town, as the valley widens, it gets higher and hotter which favors the heat-tolerant Zinfandel grapes which are planted like shrubs in a line by the old Italian American families. These northern valleys are becoming too hot for the beloved Cabernet grape, so wineries are experimenting with other heat-loving varietals. This upper valley is wide, but not so long and the wineries are more spread out, which gives the place a relaxed feel, quite different from the often-congested areas to the south.

In between the destination wineries are numerous smaller premium producers. Starting at Saint Helena, on Highway 29 is Trinchero Family Estate's expansive property with its elegant tasting room and culinary center. Brasswood Cellars is a tasting room and complex of special note because it includes a custom crush facility, a bakery and deli, as well as a full dining restaurant. Across the way is charming, biodynamic and artistic Ehlers Estate. Other notable wineries are Markham Vineyards with its photography gallery and Freemark Abby Winery with its long history and new Roadhouse Eatery, followed small, rustic Tudal Winery on the same road as the lovely Benessere Vineyards, specializing in Italian varietals.

A pretty winery on the Silverado Trail is Titus Vineyards with their relaxing patio, and well-known Duckhorn Vineyards with their extensive outdoor porch seating around their Craftsman style mansion. Then there is the hilltop classic Rombauer

Wineries Close to Calistoga

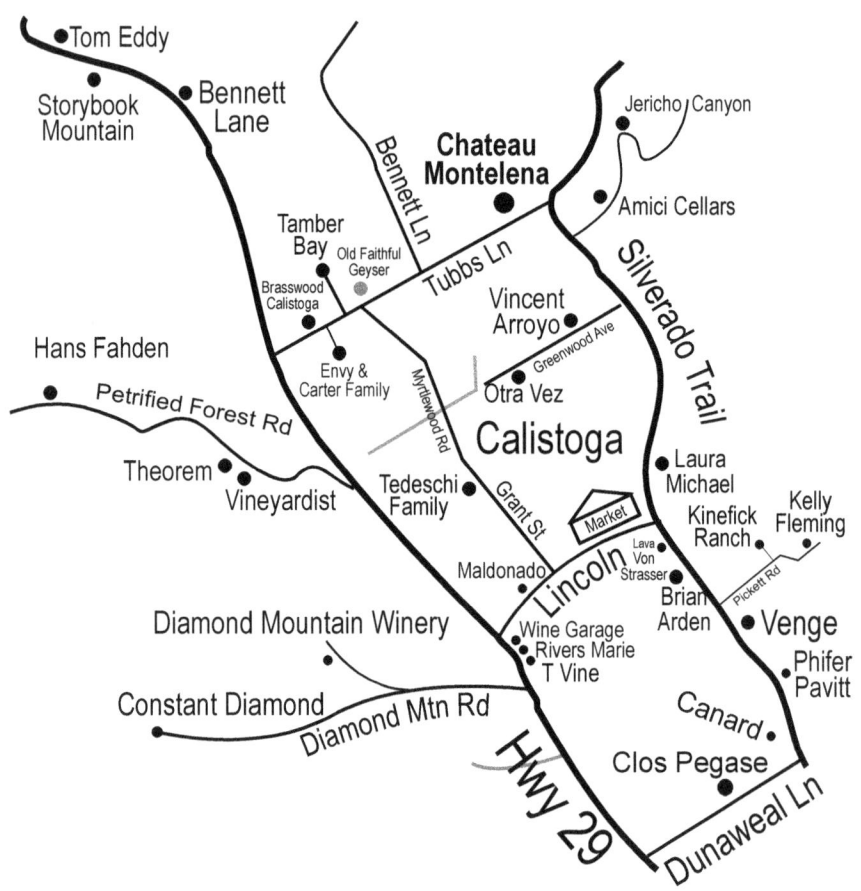

Vineyards, perched atop their caves, and Failla Wines with their cottage and cave tastings of their Sonoma coast Pinots and Chardonnays, rare varietals for this part of the valley.

Standing in the middle of vineyards, the modern, industrial-looking Mending Wall Winery is remarkable. Paoletti Estate Winery is fancier outside than in, except in their sculpture cave. Look for the Italian flag flying by their entrance. Venge Vineyards has that industrial look that belies their good wines. Just before downtown Calistoga on Silverado Trail is Brian Arden Wines, a family winery that sources their grapes from their vineyards up the road in Lake County. This part of the valley was hit hard during the 2020 Glass Fire, which damaged the Fairwinds and Dutch Henry wineries, among others.

On the crossroads just south of Calistoga are a group of excellent wineries, starting with Frank Family Vineyards, a popular place with stellar wines, lovely tasting patios, picnic grounds and a Craftsman style building. Across the street, Larkmead Vineyards makes spectacular wines, poured in an elegant setting, and at the end of the crossroad is Twomey Napa Valley where you will find excellent Merlot along with Pinot and Sauv Blanc. Clo Pegase Winery started as a home for the then owner's art collection. No art remains but it is still interesting. Across the way equally the large and blocky Girard Winery building has a pleasant, expansive tasting room and patio.

At the top of the valley, Calistoga feels like exactly what it is, an authentic old west, former cowboy town filled with mineral hot spring spas, mud baths, small hotels, B&B's, restaurants, shopping and several large resorts just outside the downtown. The oldest spa is Indian Springs, started by Sam Brannan in the 1800's.

There is a designer sized Old Faithful Geyser north of town. Calistoga got its name when Sam Brannan was entertaining potential investors, brandy bottle in hand. While comparing this

Mount Veeder

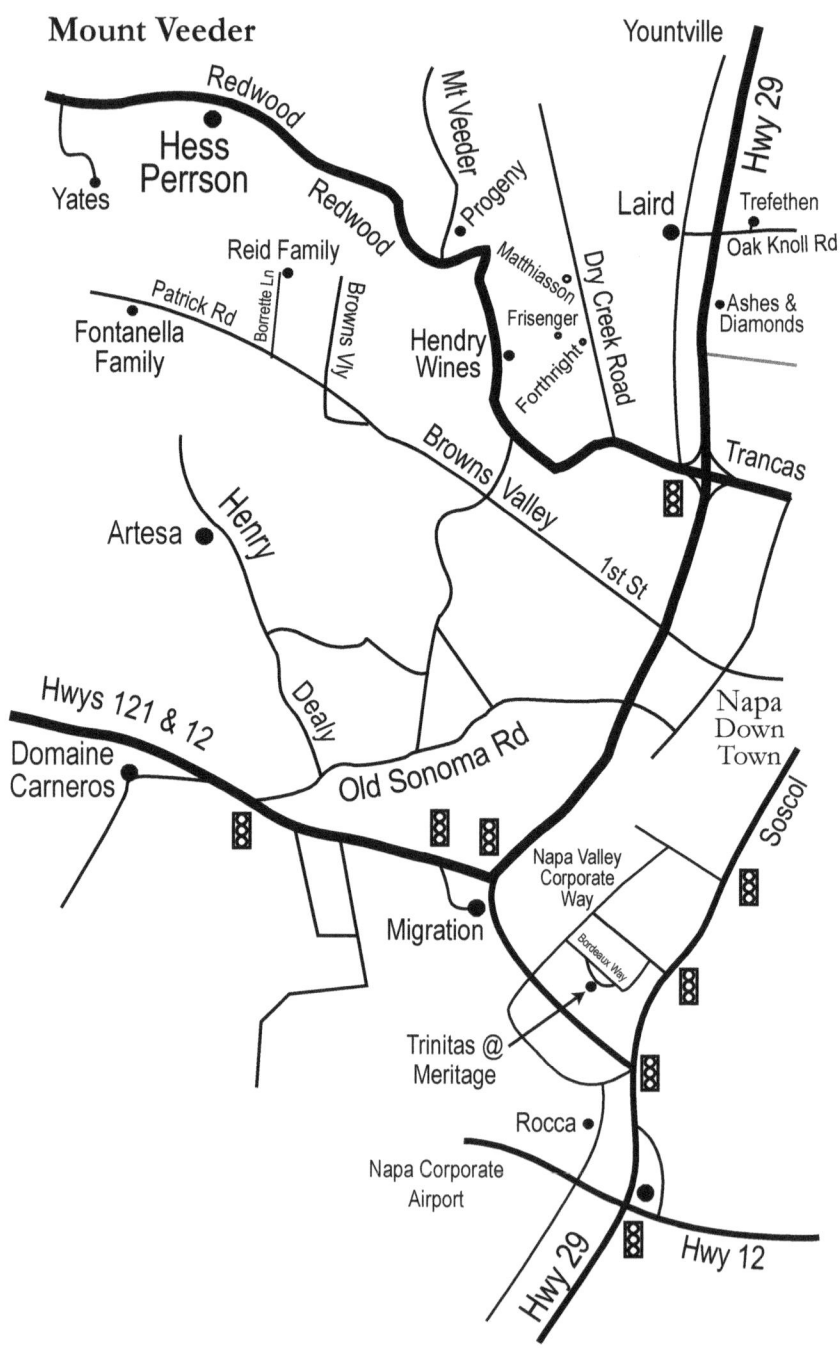

bubbling little paradise to the famous mineral springs of Saratoga, New York, he meant to call it the "Saratoga of California" but his inebriated tongue turned it into the "Calistoga of Sarafornia" and the name stuck.

North of town is the rustic but charming Tedeschi Family Winery, the tiny gem, Laura Michael Wines and steadfast Vincent Arroyo Winery. On Tubbs Lane, along with Chateau Montelena Winery, are Summers Winery, Envy Wines and Tamber Bey Vineyards whose tasting room is surrounded by idyllic horse corrals and a nearby stable. Further north, on Route 128 heading towards Northern Sonoma's Knights and Alexander Valleys, are the delightful Bennett Lane Winery and the hillside Storybook Mountain Vineyards, whose caves date back farther than historic Schramsberg. We've omitted dozens of tiny wineries. Look for them in the directory and on the reference maps.

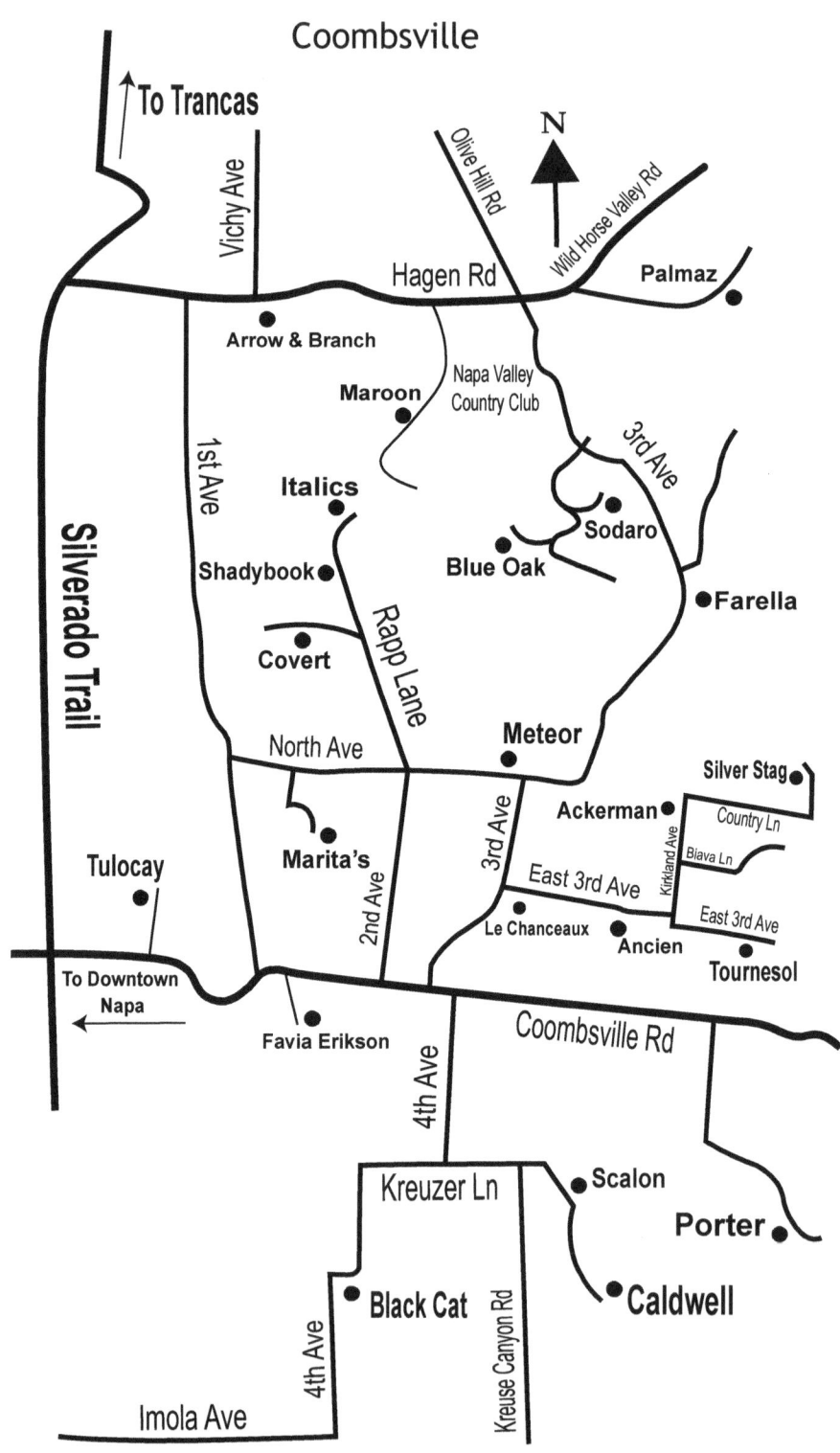

Chapter 5: The Canyons & Mountains

Farming grapevines is hard work, which is why most of the vineyards are on the valley floor, where the battle against gravity is a fair fight. But vineyards are also located in steep canyons, hillsides and mountaintops for several reasons! First, the land is cheaper. Second, well drained hillsides produce smaller, flavor-concentrated grapes that the premium wineries prefer. Finally, sometimes mountaintops, with mild slopes above the fog line, are a good opportunity if you are willing to endure the extra costs and long drives. County approvals for 'out of the way' winery sites are increasingly harder to attain because narrow canyon roads during wildfire season can become impassable. But there are plenty of small, out of the way wineries, often with spectacular views, that are worth the ride to visit. Here are those regions in Napa, starting from the south.

Mount Veeder

This southern tip of the Mayacamas mountains above Los Carneros is heavily wooded, with narrow roads through deeply shaded canyons and slopes. It is northwest of downtown Napa, and Redwood Road west off Highway 29 is the quickest route there. Alternately, coming from the south on Old Sonoma Road to Buhman Avenue and Browns Valley Road will get you there with the aid of a good map. Mount Veeder is Napa's

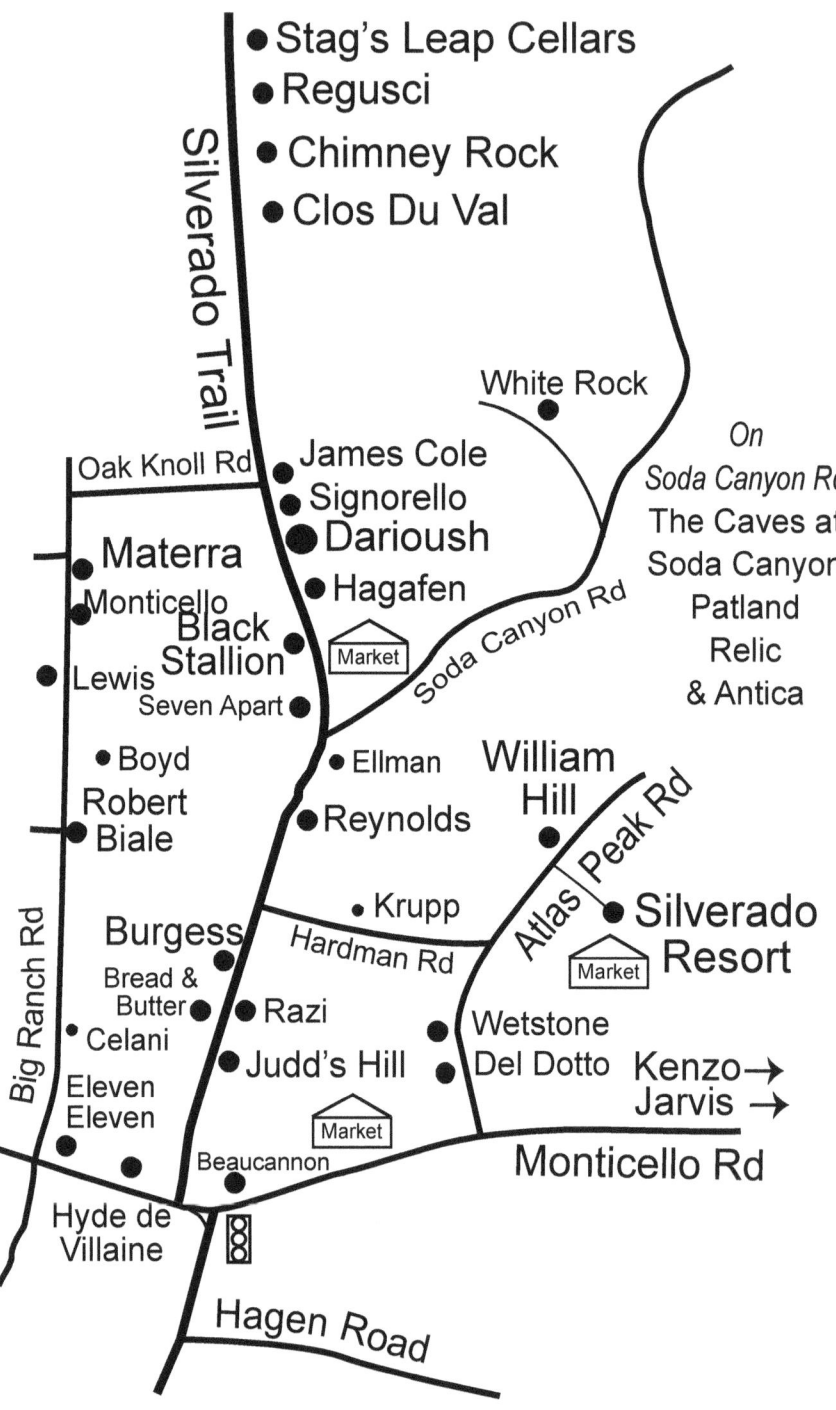

only mountainous growing region with alkaline, basalt geology. That makes wines like Cabernet gentler on the palate. These are remote vineyards and there are few wineries, with the most notable ones being the Hess Collection Winery, with their art museum, and the friendly Fontanella Family Winery.

Coombsville

Coombsville is Napa's 'newest' AVA, located east of the city's downtown. Traditionally, its lush rolling hills were for grazing livestock and even today, the Shadybrook Estate Winery is attached to a stable offering rides in the vineyard. Because the area is cool, hilly and shaded by the eastern mountains, it was considered marginal growing land. But as boutique wineries became popular, with their smaller vineyards that could be fit on a warm hillside, this area became attractive for those wanting to create something special. Numerous wineries double as second homes for wealthy owners, who employ hosts to run their hospitality. It is a lovely district, convenient to downtown Napa, filled with charming family vineyards that make wonderful wines. Originally chardonnay was the main grape, until John Caldwell put a weather station on his vineyards and found sections that would support the big money grape, Cabernet Sauvignon. Other wineries followed suit until there are now a couple of dozen premium wineries in Coombsville, open by appointment.

Soda Canyon

This narrow canyon off the Silverado Trail in the southeastern part of the valley leads to three interesting spots to visit. It was the site of a hot spring spa hotel and bottling works started in 1870's. The road is barely two lanes wide and often winds between steep hillsides and the stream. During the 2017 Atlas Peak Fire, the road became impassable and a crew of harvesters at the top of the canyon had to be airlifted out to safety by helicopter. First of these three wineries are The Caves at Soda Canyon, a partnership of four family wineries. The land was too steep and rocky for vineyards, but perfect for a cave so the entire winery is inside the mountain. The drive up is steep but well paved. Next is White Rock Vineyards on Loma Vista Drive,

Sage Canyon & Chiles Valley

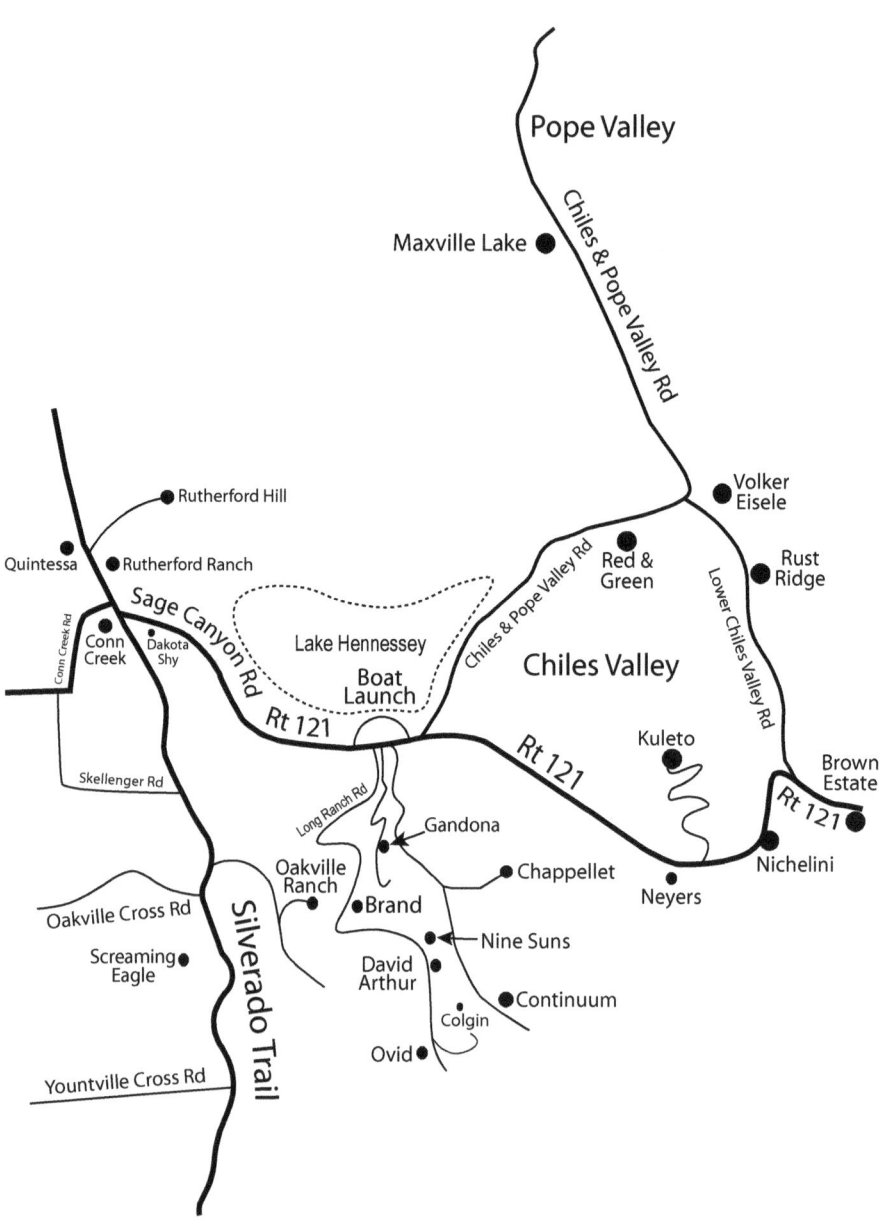

which branches off Soda Canyon Road. This land was originally planted in the 1870's and owned by the current family since the 1970's. It possesses many of the qualities of the Stags Leap District without the traffic. The third property is also the farthest and largest. Antica Napa Valley is owned by the Antinori family, an Italian wine family. It is an expansive estate with large caves and a lovely outdoor tasting area where you can enjoy the vineyard views. It is a long drive but worth the trip. Soda Canyon Road eventually leads to the Atlas Peak district and Stagecoach Vineyards owned by Gallo. The grapes are sold to numerous wineries.

Sage Canyon Road, Pritchard Hill

Mid-valley off the Silverado Trail, Sage Canyon winds east past a large reservoir. Across from the reservoir's parking lot, two roads climb ridges into the Vaca Mountains. The first is Long Ranch Road and it offers views of the Napa Valley. The wineries include Brand Napa Valley, Nine Suns, David Arthur Vineyards, Ovid Napa Valley and the ultra-premium Colgin Cellars. The second road is listed as Sage Canyon Road, but on a mailbox near the entrance is a sign for 'Pritchard Hill'. There are three notable wineries here. Gandona Winery is a small, exclusive collector's winery on a beautiful estate. The most well-known is Chappellet Winery, a family owned winery started in the 1970's, whose vineyards you pass on the way up the hill. Its wooden building was designed to blend into the surroundings. At the end of the road is Tim Mondavi's Continuum Estate. This is an extraordinary location and the only drawback is the difficulty in snagging an appointment.

Chiles Valley

Continue on Sage Canyon Road (Route 128) past the reservoir. Pope Valley Road branches off the left into that broad, high, hot valley where numerous wineries have vineyards, and it is home to a couple of small wineries. Farther along, Sage Canyon Road leads to Chiles Valley, home to the mountaintop Kuleto Estate, located behind a gate and at the end of a ridiculously long, narrow drive. The wonderful buildings and views are impressive,

Spring Mountain Wineries

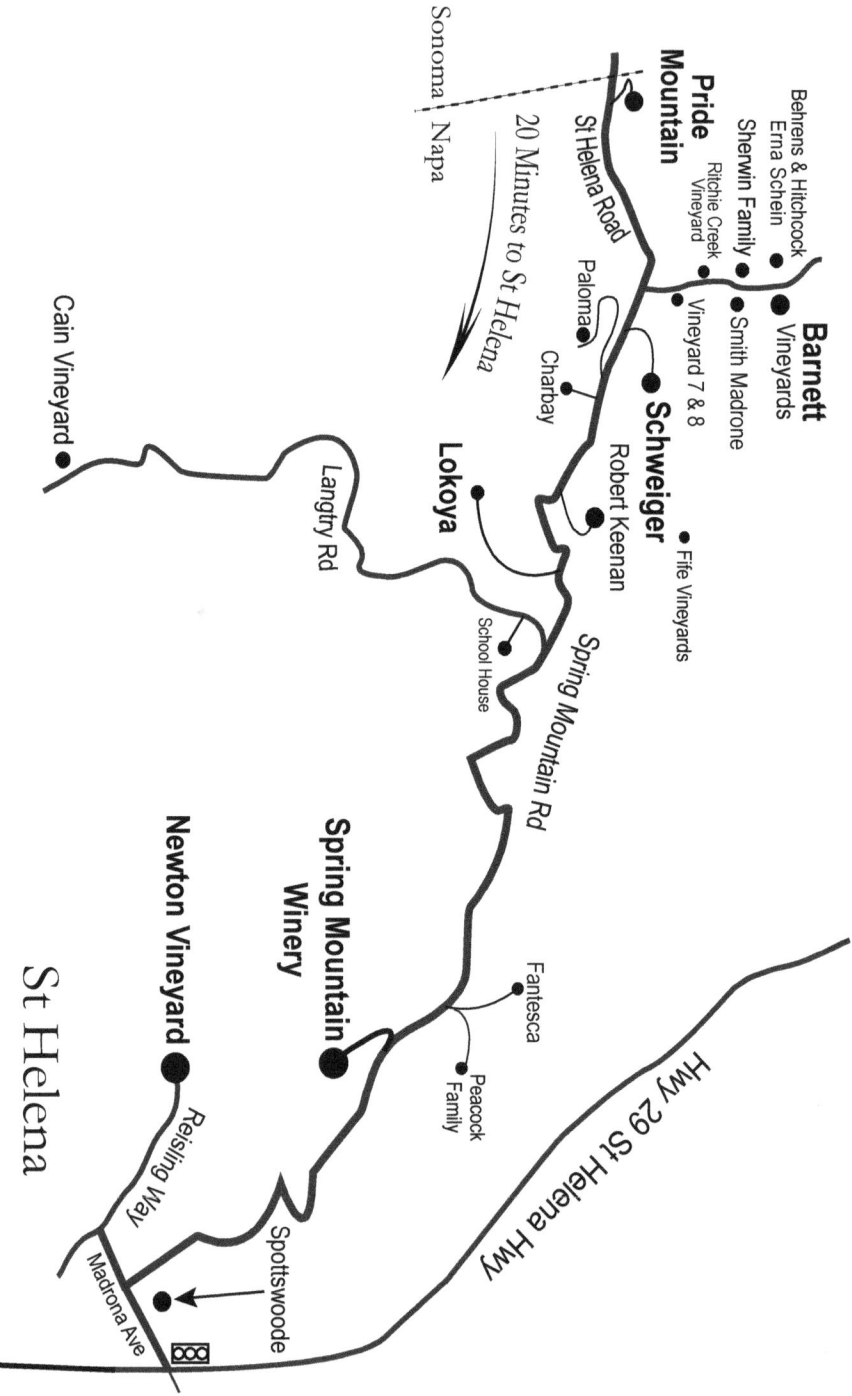

and the wines are approachable. Farther on is Napa's oldest family run winery, Nichelini Family Winery, tucked along the side of the road and rich with character.

Spring Mountain

Located conveniently northeast of downtown Saint Helena, this is Napa's most popular mountain district. From Highway 29 to the peak is a fifteen to twenty minute drive on Spring Mountain Road, which crosses the peak and connects to northern Sonoma near Santa Rosa. The first stone wineries date back to the 1800's, taking advantage of the numerous springs, eastern exposure, and sufficient altitude to keep the vines above the fog. This made it a favorite spot for small family wineries. The largest vineyard is Spring Mountain Winery, which combined three properties that span from the historic winery buildings at the base, to the mountain peak. The dozen or so wineries are mostly premiums, plus the ultra-premium Lokoya Winery. Spring Mountain Road leads to all of them except for the Newton Vineyard, which is on the southern slope, with spectacular views. Two favorites are Pride Mountain Vineyards and Schweiger Vineyards & Winery, family run wineries that sit at the top.

Howell Mountain

Located northwest of downtown Saint Helena, this is a massive, round volcanic rock. Warning: Although Howell Mountain Road connects to the Silverado Trail, do NOT take that narrow, scary road. Instead, take Deer Park Road east off the Silverado Trail. It connects to Howell Mountain Road far up the slope. On the Deer Park hillside there are four good wineries to visit including Bremer Family Winery. At the top is downtown Angwin, with its college, but don't plan on getting supplies there. Howell Mountain has about a dozen premium and ultra-premium wineries, including Cade Estate Winery, with its spectacular views, and ADAMVS, an ultra-premium, biodynamic winery that pours in a unique building. Being remote from both the ocean and the bay, above the fog line and sitting on top of thin, volcanic soils, produces wines with big, age-worthy tannins, so if that's your style, this is the place to go.

Deer Park & Howell Mountain

Chapter 6: Quick ABC's for Tasting Wine

The way you drink wine with a meal is different from how you sample it in a tasting room. The funny techniques you see people using during tastings help them perceive the wine better through the senses of sight, scent and taste. It starts with the glassware. Wineries use crystal goblets because they are rougher than glass. When you swirl the wine, those microscopic bumps pull apart its molecules, mixing them with oxygen, releasing the aromas and flavors for you to experience. Hold the glass by the stem because that makes it easier to move the wine around inside the glass. Fancier wineries have fancier glasses.

Start by holding the glass upright and taking a sniff. Much of what you're smelling is alcohol rising off the liquid. Next, set the glass on the tabletop, place your fingers firmly on top of the base and vigorously swirl the wine. Now, pick the glass up and hold it at a 45-degree angle and put your nose on the glass' lower lip, and take a sniff. Because the alcohol fumes are rising in the globe and slipping out the upper edge, bypassing your nose, you're smelling the pure fruit flavors below, the wonderful scent of fermented grapes! Sip the wine and move it around your mouth, so it touches all your taste buds from the tip of your tongue to the valley in its center, and then, both sides.

Once the flavors are well dispersed, swallow the sip. Repeat this process until there is none left. Note that there are scent notes that are only released when they touch your tongue. To access them, gently breathe in through your mouth so the aromas on your palate reach your nose via the back of your throat. There is another quality you should note called 'mouth feel'. It is how the texture of the wine feels to the surface of your mouth. Is it sharply acidic, soothingly silky, or almost sticky and syrupy? One 'mouth feel' to watch out for is the almost flame-like touch of a high alcohol, dry wine, which is why that kind of wine is called 'hot'. Port is also high in alcohol, but the wine is heavy and sweet, so the alcohol is deeply embedded in the flavors. But, many Zinfandels and Cabernets are very hot, at 15% to 16% alcohol, while totally dry (meaning that all the grape sugar has been converted to alcohol). If the dehydrating alcohol is not well moderated and integrated into the wine, it will feel like a sip dries out your tongue and you may be thirstier after the tasting than before you began.

Wine Geek Alert! There is an odd phenomenon that happens with wines that have been aged in oak for an extended period, usually eighteen months or more. As related to me by winemakers, when you swirl the wine clockwise you will smell predominantly fruit flavors. But when you swirl counterclockwise, you will also notice the nutty, sometimes spicy flavors that come from the barrel. Why does this happen? According to Ralph's best quasi-scientific analysis, it is due to the relative efficiency of vortices. A clockwise swirl more efficiently mixes the various part of the wine together. But the less efficient counterclockwise swirl allows the layers to separate. The wooden barrel flavors are the last ones to be infused into the juice and in this less organized mix, some of those woody notes are left floating at the top for your nose to discover. This technique is used by some winemakers to determine a barrel's influence on the wine. If you have a good sense of smell, you will notice the difference. Now you are officially a Wine Geek!

Chapter 7: The Winery Directory

Ackerman Family – Downtown Napa tasting from Coombsville Vineyards – Cabernet Sauvignon, Sauvignon Blanc, Blends – 608 Randolph St, Napa, CA 94559 – www.ackermanfamilyvineyards.com (855) 238–9463 – Their tastings and seminars are conducted in a beautifully restored Queen Anne Victorian mansion in downtown Napa.

Acumen Napa Valley – Downtown Napa Tasting Room – Wines: Bordeaux and Burgundy – 1315 First Street, Napa 94558 – www.acumenwine.com – (707) 492–8336 – Hours: 10:00 am – 7:00pm, closed Tues and Wed – Their vineyards are on the difficult to access Atlas peak region, which explains why a downtown tasting room was the smarter solution.

Adamvs Winery – Ultra-Premium Howell Mountain – Wines: Cabernet Sauvignon, Merlot, Blends – 555 College Rd Angwin CA 94508 www.adamvs.com – (707) 965–0555 – Hours: 9:00am – 5:00pm – This is an ultra–premium winery on the site of the old White Cottage Vineyards. They farm their land using the Biodynamic method, the highest form of organic. The wines are big and benefit from aging, because the Howell Mountain soils are thin and sit on top of a massive volcanic ball. The tasting space is as much a piece of art as it is a building.

Allora Vineyards – Small Family Winery – Wines: Cabernet Sauvignon, Petite Syrah – 3244 Ehlers Lane Saint Helena CA 94574 – www.alloravineyards.com – (707) 963–6071 – This is a small family winery where the barrel room and comfortable tasting room are below the beautiful house. The tasting is normally done by the family and their production is small, so they sell out quickly.

Alpha Omega – Fun, delicious experience – Wines: Bordeaux and Burgundy – 1155 Mee Lane Saint Helena CA 94574 – www.aowinery.com – (707) 963–9999 – Hours: 10:00am – 6:00pm – This is powerhouse winery, on a side street just off Highway 29, from which you can see their fountains soaring into the sky. When you sit outside on the tasting patio, you find yourself enjoying the cooling spray, now and then, if the wind comes from the correct quarter. They make wonderful wines, with a fantastic staff and the place is a lot of fun. They have both a tasting bar and seated tastings outside on the patio, which is the preferred experience.

Altamura Winery – Wooden Valley – Wines: Cabernet Sauvignon, Sangiovese – 1700 Wooden Valley Road Napa CA 94558 – www.altamura.com – (707) 253–2000 – Hours: Appointment – They are a premium wine maker with long ties to the Valley and a great reputation, producing about 5000 cases yearly. Their 400–acre property is located nine miles east from downtown Napa in an area with no other wineries. They are off the beaten path on the narrow, mountain route between Napa and Suisun Valley in Solano County, which has its own wonderful collection of small, reasonably priced family wineries.

Amici Cellars – Small in the Calistoga Hills – Wines: Cabernet Sauvignon, Pinot Noir, Chardonnay – 3130 Old Lawley Toll Road Calistoga, CA 94515 – www.amicicellars.com – (707) 967–9560 – Hours: Appointment – This is the hot part of the valley, but they source grapes from various regions and produce a wide selection of Cabernets. These are small lots of high scoring wines that are reasonably priced. They are in on the foothills of the Palisades to the east of downtown Calistoga.

Amizetta Vineyard –A Long Drive to beautiful destination in the eastern mountains – Wines: Cabernet Sauvignon and Blends – 1099 Greenfield Road Saint Helena CA 94574 – www.amizetta.com – (707) 963–1460 – Hours: 10:00am – 4:00pm Appointment – They are 6.1 miles from Silverado Trail at the eastern edge of the Napa Valley. This is a small winery and the family lives on the property. When you make the appointment make sure they give you instructions because it is not easy to find and there is a gate, so you may need the code. These are narrow roads and the drive up to the winery must be taken SLOWLY, so allow extra time to get there. But it is worth the ride because the tasting is usually conducted outside on their expansive patio, that sits at about 1000 feet elevation, with great views of the hillsides and Lake Hennessey.

Amulet Winery formerly Tuck Beckstoffer – Collectors – Wines: Bordeaux and Burgundy 230 North Fork Crystal Springs Road Saint Helena, CA 94574 www.amuletestate.com – (707) 200–4410 – Hours: Appointment –

Ancien Wines – Coombsville– Small with grapes from distant vineyards – Wines: Burgundy – East Napa, Ca 94581 – www.ancienwines.com – (707) 927–6594 – Hours: Appointment – Call for directions – They are an exception in warm Coombsville because they specialize in the cool weather grapes, Pinot Noir and Chardonnay. That is because their vineyards are no place nearby. They source grapes from places where these grapes thrive, Sonoma, the Central Coast and Washington State. They do a low–key tasting, in a little place that is not at all fancy but relaxed with good wines.

Anderson's Conn Valley Vineyards – Caves in the Eastern Hills Wines: Cabernet Sauvignon, Pinot Noir, Chardonnay – 680 Rossi Road Saint Helena CA 94574 – www.connvalleyvineyards.com – (707) 963–8600 – Hours: Appointment – They are 15 minutes from the Silverado Trail, up narrow winding roads, through low rolling hills to the east of the main valley. The tasting often includes a tour of the caves. It is a beautiful, off the beaten track location.

Anomaly Vineyards – Saint Helena – Small for Collectors – Wines: Cabernet Sauvignon, Bordeaux Blend – P.O. Box 741. Saint Helena CA 94574 (Call for directions) – www.anomalyvineyards.com – (707) 967–8448 – Hours: 10:00am – 4pm, Monday–Saturday Appointment – This tiny winery is conveniently located at the western edge of the town of Saint Helena on a residential street, with vines across the way. The tasting is in the cellar below the little tower style winery. The wines are priced for collectors. This was retirement project for the owners, and it is well–managed and enjoyable.

Antica Napa Valley – Antinori Family, a long ride up Soda Canyon – Bordeaux and Burgundy – 3700 Soda Canyon Road Napa, CA 94558 www.anticanapavalley.com – (707)–257–8700 Ext. 1 – Hours: Appointment – Tours – This is a large winery with older caves at the far end of the narrow, winding Soda Canyon Road, so allow extra time to get there. The winery was built years ago originally as a joint venture, but eventually, the Antinori family of Tuscany, took control and they have developed the tasting experience. What it lacks in convenience it makes up for in natural beauty.

Aonair Winery – In the Eastern Hills of Conn Valley with Great Views – 647 Greenfield Rd. Saint Helena CA – www.aonairwine.com – (707) 738-8352 – This is a small and charming family winery that is a favorite of our clients. The scenic ride winds its way up into the eastern hills, so plan extra time to get there. The wines are wonderful and the hospitality is relaxed. Aonair is Gaelic for 'One Man', which describes the job of the winemaker. Navigation Tip: First, the turn off Conn Valley Rd. onto Greenfield Rd. is heavily wooded and the signs are not obvious so take your time. Second, the only sign at the winery is the address on the left side at a curve. The driveway drops off steeply to the left so you won't see the winery from the road.

Apriori Cellar – Downtown Saint Helena tasting room – Wines: Burgundy Blends – 1432 Main Street, Saint Helena CA 94574 www.aprioricellar.com – (707) 512–0606 – Hours: Appointment – pairings – These grapes are sourced from wide ranging vineyards and then made into wine by the consulting winemaker, Phillipe Melka.

Arcudi Wines – For Collectors – Wines: Bordeaux Blends – 83 1st St, Napa, CA 94559 – www.arcudiwines.com

Artesa Winery – Spectacular View in Carneros – Wines: Burgundy, Bordeaux and Spanish – 1345 Henry Road Napa 94559 www.artesawinery.com – (707) 224–1668 – Hours: 10am –5pm Appointment for the seated tastings – They also have vineyards in Sonoma's Alexander Valley. This is a destination winery with spectacular views of Carneros and the San Pablo Bay. It was built by a Spanish wine making family. They removed the top of a hill, built the winery and replaced the top with the winery inside. It has stunning architecture, glass sculptures and splendid fountains. The spacious tasting room becomes a fun bar scene on the weekends, and there is plenty of room to spread out. There is a separate area and a patio for seated tastings. Take the tour of the caves and winery beneath your feet because it is worth seeing. From the patio you can see the DeRosa Art Preserve and the Domaine Carneros Winery. If you sit on Artesa's patio with your darling and a glass of wine, and that does not make you feel romantic, you are not doing it right.

Arkenstone Vineyards – Howell Mountain – Wines: Estate Red, Syrah, Sauvignon Blanc – 335 West Lane Angwin, CA 94508 – www.arkenstone.com – (707) 965–1020 – Hours: Appointment – They schedule a limited number of Appointment for small groups. They are located down a side road. If you expect a rustic experience, which is common on Howell Mountain, not so much. Their main tasting lounge is modern, and the winery is an industrial style cave complex where numerous wine labels are made that is worth seeing.

Arrow and Branch – Coombsville for Collectors – Wines: Bordeaux Blends – www.arrowandbranch.com – (707) 200–3640 Hours: Appointment – Culinary Wine pairing – Sourced from numerous prestigious Napa vineyards and tasted at the Brasswood custom crush winery project on Highway 29, north of Saint Helena.

Ashes and Diamonds – 4130 Howard Ln, Napa, CA 94558 (707) 666–4777– Hours: 11:00am – 7:00pm Appointment – www.ashesdiamonds.com – Wines: Bordeaux and Burgundy They are located just north of the city of Napa on the same driveway as the restaurant Don Giovanni. Because they are outside the agricultural Peserve, they can stay open later and serve food on the weekends. This was designed for the Millennial generation, stylish, big windows, minimalistic with open, social spaces and the wines are made in that palate.

Auburn James – Silverado Trail – Bordeaux and Burgundy - 1001 Silverado Trail South, Saint Helena CA 94574 – (707) 967–9100 www.auburnjames.com –– Hours 10:00am to 4:00pm Appointment – Bocce court – This is a located on a quick bend on the Silverado Trail. Its location makes it a bit hard to access, so when you visit consult the n detail and slow down well in advance of their driveway. This is a partnership between two winemakers who primarily focus on what they want to produce for their wine club. It is a pretty property tucked below the road's grade.

AXR Napa Valley – Tasting Room – Wines: Bordeaux Blends 3199 St Helena Highway North, Saint Helena, CA 94574 – www.axrnapavalley.com (707) 302–8181 – Hours: 10:00 am – 4:00 pm Appointment – This little tasting cottage north of Saint Helena has become quite popular thanks in part to a great winemaker.

Azur Wines – Coombsville – Collectors – www.stclairbrown.com – Wines: Bordeaux Blends – 190 Camino Oruga #9 Napa, CA 94558 – www.azurwines.com – (707) 812–4203 - Appointment.

B Cellars – Oakville Hospitality – Wines: Bordeaux Style – 703 Oakville Cross Rd, Napa, CA 94558 – www.bcellars.com – (707) 709-8787 – 10:00am – 5:00pm Appointment – Tours – Culinary Pairings – Oakville is the heart of the Valley and B Cellars made their home on an old horse ranch. The design is sleek and created for hospitality, built around a commercial kitchen that makes food pairings. They have lovely grounds with playful, figurative sculptures. Their tours include their caves, which were designed for events.

Back Stage Vineyards – Oak Knoll District Family Winery – Wines: Cabernet Sauvignon, Pinot Noir, Chardonnay – 4162 Big Ranch Rd, Napa, CA 94558 – www.backstagewines.com – (707) 637-4030 – Hours: 10:00am – 5:00pm Appointment – This is new facility and tasting room for a winery that has been making wine and pouring it at their other tasting rooms in the bay area. High quality from small vineyards.

Baldacci Vineyards – Stags Leap District Family Winery – Wines: Cabernet Sauvignon, Pinot Noir – 6236 Silverado Trail Napa CA 94558 – www.baldaccivineyards.com – (707) 944-9261 – Hours: 10:00am – 5:00pm Appointment – This family-run winery is tucked into a southern facing hillside, surrounded by some of Napa's most famous labels. In 2021 they expanded their caves and built a new hospitality building.

Ballentine Vineyards – Wines: Cabernet Sauvignon, Chenin Blanc, Zinfandel, Merlot, Cabernet Franc, Syrah, Petite Syrah, Petit Verdot – 2820 St Helena Highway North Saint Helena CA 94574 – www.ballentinevineyards.com – (707) 963-7919 – Hours: 10:00am – 4:00pm Appointment – This fourth generation family vineyards and winery is under stated, but they make good value wines from their own grapes and pour them in a cute, compact tasting room on their patio overlooking their vineyards. The sign is primarily visible as you are traveling north.

Barnett Vineyards – Premium Spring Mountain Views – Wines: Cabernet Sauvignon, Pinot Noir, Chardonnay – 4070 Spring Mountain Road Saint Helena CA 94574 – www.barnettvineyards.com – (707) 963-7075 – Hours: 10:00am – 4:00pm Appointment – A charming, family winery clinging to the side of Spring Mountain with incredible views from the tasting patios built into the hillside. Plan well in advance.

Beaucanon Estate – Wines: Bordeaux and Burgundy – 1006 Monticello Road, Napa – www.beaucanonestate.com – (707) 254-1460 Hours: 10:00am – 4:00pm Appointment – Wines: Cabernet blends and Chardonnay. The Longwood Ranch vineyards owned by the Bordeaux de Conick family, was part of Salvador Vallejo's 1850's land grant. They have been making good quality, reasonably priced wine there for twenty years. They do limited tastings and can be hard to reach.

Beaulieu Vineyard – Grand Rutherford Winery – Wines: Cabernet Sauvignon, Chardonnay, Pinot Noir, Merlot, Zinfandel, Syrah, Sauvignon Blanc, Shiraz, Sangiovese, Viognier, Port, Blends – 1960 St Helena Highway (Highway 29). Rutherford 94559 – www.bvwines.com – (707) 967-5230 – Hours: 10:00am – 5:00pm – This is one of Napa's grand old wineries that survived Prohibition, thanks to the owner, Georges de Latour, providing sacramental wines to the Catholic churches thanks to his friend, the Archbishop of San Francisco. Prohibition was wonderful for church membership and the winery expanded to a million cases a year over that thirteen-year period. French for 'What a beautiful place', describes the original winery location across from Frog's Leap. They make both good value and premium wines. The main tasting room offers a wide line of wines, while the Reserve building, with its patio, pours the revered George de La Tour Reserve, produced since 1936. The reserve was started by Andre Tchelistcheff, the source of many winemaking innovations used internationally today. That is his statue outside the reserve room. Known as 'BV'.

Bell Wine Cellars – Fine Wines by Yountville – Wines: Cabernet Sauvignon, Syrah, Port, Chardonnay, Zinfandel, Viognier, Merlot, Sauvignon Blanc. 6200 Washington Street Yountville CA 94599 – www.bellwine.com – (707) 944-1673 – Hours: 10:30am to 4:00pm Appointment – This is a small, classy winery south of Yountville. The tasting is in the winery tank room or seated in one of the side rooms. The tour includes the vineyards and winery. They have a loyal clientele so much of their wine is shipped directly to their customers. The grounds are nice although mostly intended for the use of the wine club during events.

Benessere – Italian Varietals North of Saint Helena – Wines: Pinot Grigio, Sangiovese, Syrah, Zinfandel, Pinot Noir, Muscat di Canelli, Super Tuscan style – 1010 Big Tree Road Saint Helena CA 94574 – www.benesserevineyards.com – (707) 963-5853 Ext 105 – Hours: 10:00am – 5:00pm –This was founded by people who had a love of all things Italian. The name means 'Well Being' in Italian and between the beautiful location, the intimate tasting room and the wonderfully made wines that describes the place quite well.

Bennett Lane Winery – Calistoga and Worth the Ride – Navigation Tip: Their driveway is located on Highway 128, not on Bennett Lane – Wines: Chardonnay, Cabernet Sauvignon, Blends 3340 Highway 128 Calistoga CA 94515 – www.bennettlane.com (707) 942–6684 Hours: 10:00am – 5:30pm – They are at the northern tip of the Napa Valley. Besides good wines, they also have picnic tables, good views and tours that include a demonstration vineyard. Their signature wine is called Maximus after the Roman Emperor Magnus Maximus.

Beringer Vineyards – Saint Helena – History & Multiple Tours Wines: A wide variety ranging from commercial up to pricey 2000 Main Street Saint Helena 94574 – www.beringer.com (707) 967–4412 – Hours: 10am–6pm (10am – 5pm winter) Beringer is located at the north edge of downtown Saint Helena. It is one of the world's most visited wineries, but it is so spread out that it rarely feels crowded. Continuously in operation since in 1876, today the dramatic Rhine House that you can you see from the road hosts the reserve tasting, while the old winery building, hosts the general tasting and gift shop. The modern winery is across the street. They offer a wide variety of wines and tours. The most charming tasting experience is the reserve, because the building is gorgeous, patterned after the family home in Germany. Many of these Mansion wines are sold only at the winery, so if you have an impression of Beringer as 'white Zinfandel', be prepared to have that idea knocked out of the park. The grounds are great for strolling.

Blackbird Vineyards – Oak Knoll Merlot tasted in Downtown Napa Wines: Bordeaux and Burgundy – 831 Latour Court, Suite B1 – www.blackbirdvineyards.com – (707) 252–4444 – Hours: Appointment – The vineyards are located at Big Ranch Road and Oak Knoll Cross Road. Their name comes from the local patois in France, where Merlot means blackbird.

Black Cat Vineyard – Coombsville – Wines: Syrah, Cabernet Sauvignon, Zinfandel – 1352 4th Ave, Napa, CA 94559 – www.blackcatvineyard.com – (707) 321–0866 – This is a small family winery where the owner is the winemaker. She makes beautiful wines. Their own Coombsville estate vineyards were planted in the late 90's, to Syrah and Cabernet Sauvignon. But they also source fruit from vineyards in Rutherford and Howell Mountain.

Black Stallion Winery – Southern Silverado Trail – Wines: Chardonnay, Pinot Grigio, Sauvignon Blanc, Muscat Canelli, Rose', Merlot, Syrah, Cabernet Sauvignon – 4089 Silverado Trail Napa CA 94558 www.blackstallionwinery.com – (707) 253-1400 – Hours: 10:00am 5:00pm – This stone building was previously an equestrian center which explains the statue at the entrance. They are conveniently located on the southern edge of the Silverado Trail minutes north of downtown Napa. They have a spacious, beautifully appointed tasting room, including wonderful seating areas for special tastings and a comfy room just for the wine club. To the side they have a spacious outdoor tasting area complete with a bar. Nearby are the Reynolds Family winery, Darioush and Luna. Navigation Tip: Enter by the driveway directly in front of the winery because it is more dramatic. That brings you around to the back where you will find the entrance.

Blankiet Estate – Stunning Yountville Estate – 2358 California Dr, Yountville, CA 94599 – www.blankiet.com – (707) 963-2001 – Appointment – This hillside estate sits above the Dominus vineyards on the Mayacamas mountain slopes. It is directly east of downtown Yountville. This is an elegant property in a building that resembles a French castle. The caves and tasting room are classic. The only challenge is that their production does not equal the demand, so the wine is available via their waiting list. With that said, the property is so special that it is well worth the visit.

Blue Oak – Coombsville Collectors – Wines: Chardonnay, Merlot and a Bordeaux Blend – 44 Blue Oak Ln, Napa, CA 94558 – www.blueoakvineyard.com – (707) 253-1382 – This is a little vineyard that produces high quality wines that are reasonably priced compared to some of their neighbors. Because of the combination of prices and quality the wines are mostly available by allotment. They do not do many tastings, but for the collector this is a good place to visit.

Boeschen Vineyards – Saint Helena – Wines: Bordeaux Blends 3242 Silverado Trail North Saint Helena, CA 94574 www.boeschenvineyards.com – (707) 963-3674 – Hours: 10:00 am – 3:30pm Appointment – he classic Bordeaux grapes including a Petite Verdot. The location is pretty and doing the tasting with the wine maker is always special. They do limited tastings so schedule well in advance. They are south of Rombauer and Failla.

Boich Family Cellar – for Collectors – Wines: Bordeaux – 651 Wall Rd, Napa, CA 94558 –www.boichfamilycellar.com –

(707) 254–8500 Hours: Appointment – At Hunnicutt.

Bouchaine Vineyards – Carneros Views – Wines: Chardonnay, Pinot Noir, Pinot Gris, Syrah, Pinot Meunier, Gewürztraminer 1075 Buchli Station Road Napa CA 94559 – www.bouchaine.com – (707) 252–9065 – Hours: 10:30 – 5:00pm Appointment. This is one of the jewels of Los Carneros. In 2019 they opened a new hospitality building overlooking the original tasting room, which they continue to use for walk-in tastings. The wines are elegantly made, and you should visit early in the day when your taste buds are fresh. Once you taste big Napa Cabernets your palate will be too saturated to appreciate the subtle flavors of Pinot and Chardonnay.

Bounty Hunter Bar and Restaurant – 975 1st St, Napa, CA 94559 Wines: A wide variety – www.bountyhunterwinebar.com – We've included this because it is more than just a bar, they also produce their own wines. They offer an amazing array of wines by the glass, so you can taste many of the local standouts. They also have a fun menu that goes well with wine. It is in downtown Napa near the corner of First and Main. Page 42

Boyd Family Vineyards – Oak Knoll – Wines: A wide variety including a great Rose – 4042 Big Ranch Road, Napa CA 94558 – www.boydwine.com – (707) 254–7353 – This is a small family winery that mostly sells their wine via the web and to their wine club. The wines are high quality and reasonably priced. They are next door to the Biale winery by the intersection of Salvador Avenue and Big Ranch Road. They are not normally open to visits but if you are interested in their wines give them a call next time you are in the valley.

Brand Napa Valley – Sage Canyon Collectors – Wines: Bordeaux Blends – 90 Long Ranch Rd, St Helena, CA 94574 – www.brandnapavalley.com – (707) 963–1199 – Hours: Appointment This is an premium winery at a bend of the road up to the ridge that overlooks the valley. The hospitality space is gracious and done in a western theme, complete with saddles and horseshoes, hence brand! When you arrive, they open the.

Brasswood Cellars – Food, Wine and Events in Saint Helena - 3111 Saint Helena Highway North, Saint Helena, CA 94574 – www.brasswood.com (707) 968–5434 – Hours: 10:00am – 5:00pm – Bar and Restaurant: 11:30am – 9:00pm – Cafe Market and Bakery: 9:00am – 5:00pm. Unlike most Napa wineries they can have food and a winery together because they are in a commercial zone. So, they have all the features of V. Sattui, without the crazy crowds because they are north of downtown Saint Helena. Their own wines are good and reasonably priced. Their winery is a custom crush facility that serves small labels, that are poured in the facility's tasting areas.

Bravante Vineyards – Howell Mountain Cave Tasting – Wines: Bordeaux – 300 Stone Ridge Road Angwin CA – www.bravantevineyards.com – (707) 965–2552 – Hours: Appt.

Bread and Butter – 3105 Silverado Trail, Napa, CA 94558 – www.breadandbutterwines.com – (833) 332-7323 – This large production winery opened a new premium tasting room in 2021 on the southern edge of the Silverado Trail. They are using local grapes and a local winemaker. It is convenient and the wines are well made and priced.

Bremer Family Winery – Deer Park Appointment – Wines: Cabernet Sauvignon, Merlot, Zinfandel, Cabernet Franc, Claret, Petite Syrah, Port, White Port – 975 Deer Park Road Saint Helena CA 94574 – www.bremerfamilywinery.com – (707) 963–5411 – Hours: 10:00am to 5:00pm – They are tucked on the hillside of Howell Mountain. The tastings are mostly either on the patio or in the winery depending on the weather. It is low key with good wines. The old wine building was restored and tied into their newer caves.

Brian Arden Wines – 331 Silverado Trail N, Calistoga, CA 94515 (707) 942–4767 – Hours: 11:00am – 4:30pm Appointment – www.brianardenwines.com – While they are located on the Silverado Trail, they are inside the Calistoga city limits. The family are grape growers in Lake County. They make lovely wines and pour them in a modern setting designed for relaxing.

Brown Estate – Downtown Napa Tasting Room – Wines: Bordeaux, General French Blends – 1005 Coombs Street Napa CA – www.brownestate.com – (707) 963–2435 – Hours: Appointment 11:00am – 7:00pm – Estate Tours for members.

Buehler Vineyards – Conn Valley Appointment – Wines: Cabernet Sauvignon, Chardonnay, Zinfandel, White Zinfandel - 820 Greenfield Road., Saint Helena CA 94574 – www.buehlervineyards.com – (707) 963–2155 – Hours: 10:00am – 4:00pm Appointment – Founded 1978, it is 20 minutes from the Silverado Trail to reach this isolated winery, but they make some good wines, that are reasonably priced.

The tour is conducted by a family member and the whole experience is informative and relaxed. If you want something off the beaten path and want to stock your cellar this is the place for you.

Buoncristiani Family Winery – At the Soda Canyon Caves – Bordeaux and Burgundy Blends – 2275 Soda Canyon Rd, Napa, CA 94558 – www.buonwine.com – (707) 259-1681 – Hours: 10am – 4:30pm Appointment – Wonderful wines.

Buhman Ranch – Wines: Bordeaux and Burgundy – 1331 Buhman Ave, Napa, CA 94558 – www.buhmanwines.com – (707) 227-7078 Hours: Appointment – This is a rustic cattle ranch and vineyard in the northern part of Los Carneros that offers some nice wines.

Burgess Cellars – New Location – Wines: Cabernet Sauvignon, Merlot, Syrah – 2921 Silverado Trail Napa CA 94558 - www.burgesscellars.com – (707) 963-4766 ?– Hours: Appointment – The 2020 Glass fire destroyed their buildings on the Deerpark slopes, so they bought the Luna facility on the southern Silverado Trail and opened there in July of 2021. It is much more convenient. Their Deerpark vineyards were first planted in the 1880's and Burgess started in 1972, when there were less than 30 wineries in Napa. They changed ownership right before the Glass fire.

Cade Winery – Beautiful Views on Howell Mountain – Wines: Cabernet blend, Sauvignon Blanc/Semillon. 360 Howell Mountain Road South Angwin CA 94508 – www.cadewinery.com – (707) 945-1220 – Hours: Appointment – This state of the art, LEEDS winery perched on the mountainside, enjoys spectacular valley views. The experience feels formal but the winery and caves are part of the tour. They are surprisingly more famous for the views and architecture than the wines.

Cade13th Vineyard — Howell Mountain – Formerly the site of Ladera – Wines: Cabernet Sauvignon, Blends – 150 White Cottage Road South Angwin CA 94508 – www.cadewinery.com – (707) 965-2445 – Hours: Appointment – The original building was constructed in 1886 and transformed, rather than restored, by the new owners in 2000, by keeping the exterior stone walls and creating a new intra-structure to hold the winery equipment. It is an innovative approach. In 2018–19 the Plumpjack group purchased it and added their vineyards. .

Cain Vineyard and Winery – Spring Mountain – The 2020 Glass fire completely destroyed their buildings but the vineyards were spared.

Check the website – Wines: Bordeaux - 3800 Langtry Road Saint Helena CA 94574 – www.cainfive.com – (707) 963–1616 Hours: Appointment – They are halfway up Spring Mountain Road, and along narrow, winding Langtry Road. But they have great views and wonderful wines. They do limited tastings so plan well in advance.

Cakebread Cellars – Popular Appointment Winery – Wines: Sauvignon Blanc, Chardonnay, Pinot Noir, Merlot, Syrah, Zinfandel, Cabernet Sauvignon, – 8300 Saint Helena Highway (Highway 29). Rutherford CA 94573 – www.cakebread.com – (800) 588–0298 – Hours: 10:00am – 4:00pm Appointment - This family winery, with the easy to remember name, did several expansions over the years to create a wonderful hospitality experience surrounded by vines on the broad valley floor. They offer numerous classes. They are located on the lines between the Rutherford and Oakville AVA's north of Mondavi. Navigation Tip: Going north on Highway 29 they are just past the Turnbull winery that looks very similar.

Calafia Cellars – Small – Wines: Bordeaux and Burgundy - 629 Fulton Lane Saint Helena CA 94574 – www.calafiacellars.com – (707) 963–0114 – Hours: 11:00am – 5:00pm – Hours: Appointment – The owner/winemaker has some serious winemaking chops, having honed his skills at Souverain, Mayacamas, Stag's Leap Vineyard and Hess Collection. They are small production of a red table wine in the Bordeaux style.

Caldwell Vineyards – Winery Caves in Coombsville – Wines: Bordeaux and Burgundy – 169 Kreuzer Lane Napa CA 94559 – www.caldwellvineyard.com – (707) 255–1294 – Hours: Appointment – Located in the hills to the east of the city of Napa. The winery is inside a thirty thousand square feet cave complex used by numerous labels. There are great views of the city of Napa in the distance. The ride down to the cave is on a steep gravel drive cut into the hillside so take your time. The vineyards you pass on the way sit above the caves. The tasting experience is fun, but for the enthusiast.

Canard Vineyard – Calistoga – Wines: Bordeaux Blends – 1016 Dunaweal Lane Calistoga CA 94515 – www.canardvineyard.com – (707) 942–1149 – Hours: 10:30 am – 4:30pm by Appointment – Check for their tasting location since their previous, Fairwinds Estate, was destroyed in the 2020 Glass Fire that hit the north valley.

Cardinale Estate Wines – Serious Ultra-Premium Experience Wines: Cabernet Sauvignon blends – 7600 St Helena Highway (Highway 29). Oakville CA 94562 – www.cardinale.com – (707) 948–2643 – Hours: 10:30–5 Appointment – This long, stone building sits on a low hill on the east side of the road north of Yountville across from Far Niente. The tasting takes place in a classic conference room with the wine educator. They make great red wines with an exclusive feel. This is the old Pepi winery, now owned by the Jackson Family, the owner of Kendall Jackson. When you are standing in the parking lot look to the east, you will see the top of an extensive artificial cave complex which is a Jackson Family winery facility.

Carter Cellars – Calistoga – Wines: Bordeaux Blends – 1170 Tubbs Ln Calistoga, CA 94515 – www.cartercellars.com – (707)445–0311 Hours: 10:00am – 4:30pm Monday – Sunday Appointment – They share a space with Envy Wines.

Castello di Amorosa – Northern Napa's Castle with Tours – Wines: Multiple from dry to sweet. 4045 North St Helena Highway (Highway 29). Calistoga 94515 – www.castellodiamorosa.com – (707) 967–6272 – Hours: 9am–6pm, 9am – 5pm November–February – People laughed when we called Napa Valley Disneyland for adults, and then this 12th century Tuscan–style castle/winery with 110 rooms, complete with dungeon, called "Castle of the Beloved" opened after 13 years of work. It has become one of Napa's most visited wineries and the tours are fun. Hint: You can rent the dungeon for Halloween. Now that is one party your friends will not forget! They offer guided and self–guided tours. Appointments are suggested and you cannot enter without paying. Castles are cold in winter and cool in summer, so dress accordingly. Children are restricted to certain tours and there are too many stairs for babies and strollers. It is surrounded by vines, olive trees, chickens and the occasional sheep. Drive up and see the outside even if you do not plan to go in. They suffered damage in the 2020 Glass Fire.

Cathiard Family Estate – Rutherford at the west end of Zinfandel Lane. 1978 – Red Blends – W. Zinfandel Lane St. Helena CA 94574 – (707) 302-5503 www.cathiardvineyard.com –This historic property, with its stone winery, was perviously Flora Springs. In 2020 it was sold to a French family. It is a lovely property with views. The vineyards are being converted to Biodynamic and a new winery was constructed,

Caves at Soda Canyon – Multiple Wineries – Wines: Bordeaux and Burgundy Blends – 2275 Soda Canyon Rd, Napa, CA 94558 www.thecavesatsodacanyon.com – (707) 259–1681 – Hours: 10am 4:30pm Appointment – They are built into the top of the ridge overlooking the Stags Leap district, so expect a steep drive, but great views. The tasting takes place in the cave, and they feature the wines of the five partner wineries.

Caymus Vineyards – Famous Red – Navigation Tip: At the junction of Conn Creek, Skellenger and Rutherford Roads. Be early for your appointment. Wines: Cabernet Sauvignon, Zinfandel, Sauvignon Blanc, Chardonnay – 8700 Conn Creek Road Rutherford CA 94573 – www.caymus.com – (707) 967–3010 – Hours: 10:00am – 4:00pm – They are a premium winemaker with a great reputation and a favorite at restaurants. They do a seated tasting. Make sure you arrive early because they may give your spot away. In nice weather they do their tastings outside. They also have a tasting bar, and in wet weather they move into the barrel rooms, which are drafty, so bring a jacket. Navigation Tip: They are at the junction of Conn Creek, Skellenger and Rutherford Roads behind a foliage covered wall.

Ceja Vineyards – 22989 Burndale Road Sonoma, CA 95476 www.cejavineyards.com – (707) 255–3954 – Hours: 11am – 5pm – Their vineyards are in both Napa and Sonoma counties and their tasting room is accessible on Carneros Highway.

Celani Family Vineyards – Oak Knoll Collectors – Wines: Bordeaux and Burgundy – 2230 Big Ranch Road, Napa CA 94558 – www.celaniwines.com – (707) 255–5645 –Hours: Appointment - This private tasting for the Cabernet collector is in a Tuscan style home surrounded by vineyards, north of Trancas Street. They just north of Trancas Street, the cith of Napa's northern commercial road and the Eleven Eleven winery. They are just south of Biale, Corley Family and Materra.

Chappellet Winery and Vineyard – Sage Canyon Appointment Wines: Cabernet Sauvignon, Merlot, Cabernet Franc, Chardonnay, Chenin Blanc, Cuvee – 1581 Sage Canyon Road Saint Helena CA 94574 – www.chappellet.com – (707) 963–7136 – This is a world class, family run winery on the slopes of Pritchard Hill off Sage Canyon Road, east of the main valley. Started in 1967 they chose a perfect location for growing. These mountain roads are small and winding, so get directions. Allow twenty minutes from the Silverado Trail to their front door, which is at the near end of the winery buildings. Stay on the path to avoid the poison oak. Navigation Tip: On Sage Canyon Road there is a sign for Pritchard Hill on a mailbox that marks the turn. Driving east it is the third of three roads across from the parking lot by Hennessy Lake. As you go up the mountain take your time. After you go through a vineyard area with great views you will see small signs for the winery.

Charles Krug Winery – Great History – Wines: Cabernet Sauvignon, Merlot, Sauvignon Blanc, Chardonnay, Pinot Noir, Zinfandel, Cabernet Franc, Syrah – 2800 St Helena Highway North (Highway 29) Saint Helena CA 94574 – www.charleskrug.com (707) 967–2229 – Hours: 10:30am – 5:00pm Appointment. This is Napa's oldest operating winery, owned by Peter Mondavi's family. It was originally bought by the Mondavi family after WWII, but in the 1960's Robert Mondavi left and started his own eponymous winery. The impressive old winery building is where the tastings take place. They have an Italian style deli and coffee bar inside, so you can get food pairings with your wine. Tastings are done inside and out under the trees. The family owns some vineyards up and down the Napa Valley.

Charter Oak Winery – Tiny Downtown Saint Helena – Wines: Bordeaux, General French – 831 Charter Oak Ave, St Helena, CA 94574 www.charteroakwine.com – (707) 963–2298 – Hours: 10:00am – 4:30pm – Hours: Appointment – Art Gallery. This winery lives in the basement of a house, part of the tradition of home Italian winemakers who once filled the area.

Chase Cellars - Saint Helena - Small and Charming with interesting wines - 2252 Sulphur Springs Ave, St Helena, CA 94574 - chasecellars.com - (707) 963-1284 - This family owned winery is located just south of downtown Saint Helena on the revered Hayne Vineyard. They make Chardonnay, Zinfandel, Petite Sirah and a Cabernet Sauvignon -

Chateau Boswell – Small but Diverse Ultra–Premium – *Note: Their building are being rebuilt after the 2020 Glass fire.* – Wines: Chardonnay, Cabernet Sauvignon – 3468 Silverado Trail North Saint Helena CA 94574 – www.chateauboswellwinery.com – (707) 963-5405 – Hours: Appointment They are located on the east side of the Silverado trail north of downtown Saint Helena. Their founding winemaker was the famous Andre Tchelistcheff, and their current is Phillipe Melka, so they aim for premium to ultra-premium. They source grapes from exceptional vineyards throughout California.

Chateau Montelena Winery – Of the Judgment of Paris and Bottle Shock Fame – Wines: Chardonnay, Cabernet Sauvignon, Zinfandel, Riesling – 1429 Tubbs Lane Calistoga 94515 – www.montelena.com – (707) 942–5105 – Hours: 9:30 – 4:00pm Appointment – The winery was built into a hillside at the top of the valley in the late 1800's by the Tubbs family, as a gravity fed winery. It passed through another family that built the lake before the Barrett's began making wine there. They had only been at it a couple of years when their Chardonnay, a blend of Sonoma and Napa grapes, made a splash. It took the top score for a white wine against their American and French contemporaries at the 1976 Judgment of Paris blind tasting. Combined with the Stag's Leap Cellars win for their Cabernet, Napa suddenly became a serious player in the international wine world. They are located north of downtown Calistoga next to the Old Faithful Geyser. It is a gorgeous, classic building with remarkable grounds and a beautiful Asian style Jade Lake. The tasting room sits on top of the winery and the parking is below, so you pass the crush pad on the way up. This is fun during harvest when you will see the grape processing out front. There is a small parking lot on the upper level in case the walk up the two flights of stairs pose a problem.

Checkerboard Vineyards – Calistoga Ultra–Premium for Collectors Wines: Bordeaux Blends – 4331 Azalea Springs Way, Calistoga – www.checkerboardvineyards.com – (707) 942–4112 – Appointments.

Chiarello Family Vineyards – Downtown Inside Ottimo – Wines: An interesting variety – 6525 Washington St Yountville CA 94599 – www.chiarellovineyards.com – (707) 256–0750 – Hours: 10am–6pm Sunday 10am – 5pm – Celebrity chef Michael Chiarello's Ottimo store in Yountville has something for everyone, including his wines.

Chimney Rock Winery – Stags Leap's White Building – Wines: Cabernet Sauvignon, Fumé Blanc, Rosé of Cabernet Franc – 5350 Silverado Trail Napa CA 94558 – www.chimneyrock.com - 707) 257–2641 – Hours: 10:00am – 5:00pm Appointment - They are part of the Terlato Family Wineries who also owns Rutherford Hill Winery. They always do a good job of producing high quality wines and producing a satisfying tasting room experience. It is easy to spot from the Silverado Trail, it is a big white, South African Dutch–style building. The original owner lived in South Africa for many years. The name comes from the stone cliffs that tower over the vineyards.

Cliff Lede Vineyards – Charming Stags Leap District – Wines: Sauvignon Blanc, Cabernet Sauvignon, Claret – 1473 Yountville Cross Road Yountville CA 94599 – www.CliffLedeVineyards.com – (707) 944-8642 – Hours: 10:00am – 4:00pm Appointment – This is a charming winery on the northern edge of the Stags Leap district, just minutes from downtown Yountville. The staff is nice, the wines are excellent, the gardens and patio out back are gracious and relaxing. They have a small gift area. This is a nice place for a seated tasting with a group on a shady part of the patio. From the tasting room you can see the winery in the distance nestled against the hillside, connected to its caves. On the hillside above the winery is their associated Bed and Breakfast, the Poetry Inn.

Clos Du Val – Stags Leap District – Wines: Cabernet Sauvignon, Chardonnay, Merlot, Pinot Noir – 5330 Silverado Trail Napa CA 94558 – www.closduval.com – (707) 261-5200 – Hours: 10:00am – 5:00pm Appointment – This is a French-style winery, with good wines, a modern spacious tasting room, and extensive outdoor tasting areas. It was founded in 1972 by an American businessman and a French winemaker. They are known for their Bordeaux blends, but locally they are respected for their Pinot which they grow in the rolling hills of Los Carneros on the north side of Highway 121.

Clos Pegase Winery – Great Architecture – Wines: Chardonnay, Sauvignon Blanc, Pinot Noir, Merlot, Cabernet Sauvignon 1060 Dunaweal Lane Calistoga 94515 – (707) 942-4981 – www.clospegase.com Hours: 10:30–5:00pm – This is a dramatic building and the tasting room is tucked in the far-left corner. The building is a Michael Graves creation, although the signature colors were changed.

Conn Creek Winery – At the Crossroads – Wines: Cabernet Sauvignon, Cabernet Franc, Merlot – 8711 Silverado Trail South Saint Helena CA 94574 – www.conncreek.com – (707) 963-9100 – Hours: 10:00am – 4:00pm – This is a pleasant winery that is often missed because they are located at a busy intersection, but they make some good wines. When they first planted the vineyards, it was so rocky that they had to use explosives to break up some of the boulders. We are sure by now the sulfur taste is gone from the vines. They do a great wine blending seminar in a special room, where people can make a bottle to their taste. They remarkably assembled a startling array of barrels representing most of the sections of Napa. Being able to sample them side by side is a sure way to recognize how much location shapes flavors.

Constant Diamond Mountain Vineyard – At the Top – Wines: Cabernet Franc, Merlot, Cabernet Sauvignon – 2121 Diamond Mountain Road Calistoga CA 94515 – www.constantwine.com
(707) 942–0707 – This is a premium winery located at the top the mountain. The road is long, narrow and steep. They enjoy spectacular views and the tasting is special.

Continuum Estate – Wines: Cabernet Sauvignon, Cabernet Franc, Petit Verdot, Merlot – 1677 Sage Canyon Rd, St Helena, CA 94574 www.continuumestate.com – (707) 944–8100 – Hours: 10:00am – 4:00pm Appointment – This is an extraordinary estate on the top of the Vaca Mountains to the east of the valley with great views. This is the Tim Mondavi family winery. But it is not an easy appointment to arrange.

Corison Wines – Elegant Wines – Wines: Cabernet Sauvignon, Gewürztraminer – 987 St Helena Highway (Highway 29) Saint Helena CA 94574 – www.corison.com – (707) 963–0826 – Hours: 10:00am to 5:00pm Appointment – This is a conveniently located, small winery owned by the respected winemaker, Cathy Corison, who is known for her stellar Cabernets. The tasting is in the barrel room located inside of a pretty barn. The staff is knowledgeable and low key and the vineyards are right outside the back door.

Cosentino Winery – Next to Mustard's Grill – Wines: Bordeaux, Burgundy, Gewürztraminer, Sangiovese, Dolcetto, Tempranillo, Viognier, Dessert – 7415 St Helena Highway (Highway 29) Yountville CA 94599 www.cosentinowinery.com – (707) 944–1220 – Hours: 10:00am – 5:00pm – This ivy–covered winery is just north of Yountville. It is a high energy tasting room next to Mustard's Grill. The wines are interesting and tast and the staff is fun. They attract a younger crowd, and the modern style of the place reflects that. .

Covert Winery – Collectors in Coombsville – Wine: Bordeaux Style – 15 Chateau Lane, Napa CA 94558 www.covertestate.com – (707)337–5943 – Hours: Appointment.

Crocker and Starr – Saint Helena – Wines: Bordeaux Blends 700 Dowdell Ln, St Helena, CA 94574 – www.crockerstarr.com (707) 967–9111 – Hours: 10:00am to 3:00pm Appointment Charcuterie Artisanal Cheeses – This is an excellent winery down a road from Highway 29 by downtown Saint Helena. It is a partnership of a grower and winemaker and their experience is personal and interesting.

Crosby Roamann – Corporate Park in the Crusher District – Wines: Seriously good Bordeaux and Burgundy – 45 Enterprise Ct #6, Napa CA 94558 – www.crosbyroamann.com – (707) 266–6291 – Hours: Appointment.

Cuvaison Estate Carneros – Great Views – Wines: Pinot Noir, Cabernet Sauvignon, Chardonnay, Merlot, Syrah, Zinfandel, Port – 1221 Duhig Road Napa CA 94559 – www.cuvaison.com (707) 942–2455 Hours: 10:00am – 5:00pm Appointment – Their Carneros winery is across from Domaine Carneros. It is simple, elegant with spectacular views. Navigation Tip: Their driveway is directly across from the entrance to Domaine Carneros and the winery experiences could not be more different, considering the locations. Note: In 2021 they were starting a dramatic redo of their tasting building.

Dakota Shy Winery – Collectors – Wines: Bordeaux and Burgundy – 771 Sage Canyon Road, Saint Helena – www.dakotashywine.com – (707) 244–1184 – Hours: Appt.

Darioush – A Persian Dream – Wines: Viognier, Cabernet Sauvignon, Shiraz, Chardonnay, Merlot, Pinot Noir – 4240 Silverado Trail Napa CA 94558 – www.darioush.com – (707) 257–2345 - Hours: 10:30am – 5:00pm Appointment – Any Napa visitor from Persia must come to Darioush which is at the southern end of the Silverado Trail, south of the Stags Leap district. It is patterned after a Persian temple, with an elegant tasting bar, comfy stools and low seating around tables. The golden travertine was quarried in Iran, carved in Italy and assembled in Napa, on top of the caves. Despite its formal façade, it is a family friendly place and always seems to attract the prettiest girls at the end of the day.

Darms Lane Wine – Family Winery – Wines: Cabernet Sauvignon, Petit Verdot, Chardonnay, Pinot Noir – 150 Darms Lane Napa, CA 94558 www.darmslanewine.com – (707) 224–4200 – Hours: Appointment – This is a charming family winery that makes good wines at a proper price in the south western part of the valley. The tasting is on their patio overlooking the vines and the valley beyond.

David Arthur Vineyards – Sage Canyon Appointment – Wines: Sauvignon Blanc, Chardonnay, Merlot, Cabernet Sauvignon – 1521 Sage Canyon Road Saint Helena CA 94574 – www.davidarthur.com – (707) 963–5190 – Hours: Appointment – This is a respected producer perched on a ridge overlooking the Valley. It is one of the wineries tucked up in the hills of Sage Canyon. The tasting is relaxed, but plan well in advance.

David Fulton Winery – Wine: General French – 825 Fulton Lane, Saint Helena CA 94574 – www.davidfultonwinery.com – (707) 967-0719 – Hours: Appointment – This is tiny winery in downtown Saint Helena that goes back to the earliest wine making in the area.

Davies Vineyards – Downtown Saint Helena, Related to Schramsberg – Wines: Bordeaux and Burgundy – 1210 Grayson Ave, St Helena CA 94574 – www.daviesvineyards.com – (707) 963-5555 – Hours: 9:45am – 5:00pm Appointment – Seated Tasting, Pairings – This is a downtown winery and tasting room for the family that makes the Schramsberg sparkling wines. It is in a modern stone building in downtown Saint Helena.

Davis Estates – Calistoga Silverado Trail – 4060 Silverado Trail, Calistoga CA 94515 – www.davisestates.com – (707) 942-0700 Hours: 10:00am – 4:00pm Appointment – Food Pairings – This little winery property was once part of the Larkmead property that belonged to the family of Lillie Coit in the 1800's. It went through several owners who each worked on developing the winery, because the property is not large enough for many vines. Finally, the Davis family brought it to completion and they source excellent grapes. It is a lovely property with nice views of the valley. Do not confuse them with the Davis Family Winery of Healdsburg, or the Davies Family, the still wine label of the makers of Schramsberg.

Del Dotto Vineyards (Atlas Peak) – Historic Caves – Wines: Cabernet Sauvignon, Cabernet Franc, Merlot, Pinot Noir, Sangiovese, Zinfandel, Port – 1055 Atlas Peak Road Napa CA 94558 www.DelDottoVineyards.com – (707) 256-3332 – Hours: 11:00am – 5:00pm Appointment – This is their original Napa property. These caves on Atlas Peak Road are some of the oldest in Napa, built by the architect of Inglenook and Greystone. The Del Dotto team takes a hands-on approach and tastings are normally done as part of a tour. They love to show how various barrels influence the flavors of the wine. Both wineries, old and new, are remarkable in their own ways. The wines are popular, the tour is a lot of fun and they draw plenty of repeat visitors. They are known to pour big tastings, so either hire a driver, or have a designated driver. The interior is elaborate funk.

Del Dotto Estate Winery and Caves (Zinfandel Lane) Wines: Cabernet Sauvignon, Cabernet Franc, Merlot, Pinot Noir, Sangiovese, Zinfandel, Port. 1445 St Helena Highway (Highway 29) Saint Helena CA 94574 – www.DelDottoVineyards.com – (707) 256-3332 – Hours: 11:00am – 5:00pm Appointment – This is their second property by their vineyards near the intersection of Zinfandel Lane and Highway 29; look for the two large amphorae outside the gates. The winery is mostly underground and remarkable in an explosion of Italian marble. You walk downstairs to enter. The best experience is as part of the cave tour.

Piazza Del Dotto – Property Number Three – Wines: Cabernet Sauvignon, Cabernet Franc, Merlot, Pinot Noir, Sangiovese, Zinfandel, Port – 7466 St. Helena Highway (Highway 29) Napa, CA 94558 – www.DelDottoVineyards.com – 707-963-2134 Hours: 11:00am – 5:00pm Appointment – This is the most ambitious Del Dotto winery yet, with an expansive hospitality building with tasting bars and outdoor seating areas, extensive cave and other entertainments. It is just north of downtown Yountville.

Delectus Winery – Wines: Bordeaux and Burgundy – www.delectuswinery.com – These folks make some very good wines. They were a warehouse winery near the Napa Airport for many years. Then they took over a location in St Helana from the previous owners but ran into the shutdown, so now they available online.

Diamond Creek Vineyards - Diamond Mountain – Cabernet Blends for Collectors – www.diamondcreekvineyards.com – (707) 942-6926 – 1500 Diamond Mountain Rd, Calistoga, CA 94515 – This is a longtime premium grower on Diamond Mountain just south of Calistoga. Many years ago, they almost scandalized Napa by being the first winery to charge $100 for a bottle of wine. The prices of course have not come down. The property is a short way up the mountain and each vineyard is quite distinctive. In recent years it changed hands from the original owners. Visits often include a tour of the property, and the private tastings are done in an expansive, elegant room, with views of the very pretty vineyards.

Domaine Carneros – Elegant Sparkling Wines in Southern Napa – Wines: Brut Cuvee, Brut Rosé, Le Reve Blanc de Blancs, Pinot Noir. Wines can be ordered by the glass – 1240 Duhig Road Napa 94559 www.domainecarneros.com – (707) 257-0101 – Hours: 10:00am – 6:00pm Appointment – This chateau towers over Carneros like a birthday cake with candles alight. You cannot ignore it, and you should not because it offers one of Napa's most romantic sparkling wine experiences. The building is modeled on the Taittinger family's French chateau, with large patios and gorgeous tasting rooms. The building sits high because the winery is underneath, and they offer tours into the depths that explain the sparkling wine 'methode champenoise'. Out in back is a second winery make non–sparkling Pinot Noir, which with Chardonnay are the main grapes used for Champagne. The sit-down tasting is either outside with the great views, or inside a tasting room reminiscent of Versailles. Wines are offered by the glass and flight, which should be shared. Sparkling wines are so light and fresh they often disguise the significant amount of alcohol they contain.

Domaine Chandon – Wines: Sparkling and Still wines –
1 California Dr. Yountville 94599 – www.domainechandon.com – (707) 944–2280 – Hours: 10:00am – 5:00pm – This is by downtown Yountville, with beautiful grounds, a large tasting bar, seating areas, snacks and side dishes. Domaine Chandon was the first European owned Champagne Company to invest here in the 1970's. It is not an intimate experience. At the end of the day it turns into a bit of a party. Between its history, reputation, hospitality, tours, and great wines they continue to be one of Napa's most visited locations.

DR Stephens Estate – Collectors in a Northern Napa Cave– Wines: Cabernet Sauvignon, Chardonnay, Pinot Noir, Sauvignon Blanc – 3520 Silverado Trail North Napa, CA 94558 – www.drstephensestate.com Phone: (707) 963–2908.

Duckhorn Vineyards – A Nice Seated Tasting – Wines: Sauvignon Blanc, Merlot, Cabernet Sauvignon – 3027 Silverado Trail North Saint Helena CA 94574 – www.duckhorn.com – (707) 967–2000 – Hours: 10:00am – 4:00pm Appointment – Their beautiful craftsman–style mansion at the corner of Lodi Lane and the Silverado Trail is a great landmark. This is the narrowest part of the valley, and across from the vineyards, the stone cliffs tower above the road. They do a wonderfully relaxed, seated tasting, either in the sunny salon or out on the patios. They have a great collection of duck decoys and sculptures. The grounds are lovely with a view of the vineyards. It makes a real statement, you are in the heart of wine country.

Dutch Henry Winery – Northern Silverado Trail – *Note: Their winery building was destroyed in the 2020 Glass Fire but it did not affect their vineyards, so we expect them to rebuild.* Wines: Cabernet

Sauvignon, Syrah, Argos, Zinfandel, Pinot Noir, Cabernet Franc, Chardonnay – 4310 Silverado Trail Calistoga CA 94515 www.dutchhenry.com – (707) 942–5771 – Hours: 10:0am – 4:30pm. This small winery south of Calistoga is tucked up against the mountains on the east side of the Silverado Trail. The name comes from an old mercury miner who lived in the area. The metal was popular because it was used to refine gold and its popular name, Quicksilver contributed to the naming of the Silverado Trail.

Ehlers Estate – Small, Beautiful, Biodynamic Winery – Wines: Cabernet Sauvignon, Merlot, Sauvignon Blanc, Cabernet Franc, Zinfandel 3222 Ehlers Lane Saint Helena CA 94574 – www.ehlersestate.com (707) 963–5972 – Hours: 10:00am – 4:00pm This is a beautiful, small winery located in a great old stone barn, with an interesting tasting room. Just behind it, and visible through the windows, is the winery. Alongside it is a large shaded garden with tables and bocce courts. They have a nice staff. The wines are Biodynamic.

Eleven Eleven – Trancas Street Convenient – Wines: Bordeaux and Burgundy, General French – 620 Trancas Street, Napa CA 94558 – www.elevenelevenwines.com – (707) 224–2211 – Hours: 10:00am – 4:00pm Appointment – They are at north edge of the city of Napa. They produce wonderful wines that they pour in an elegant space that blends from inside to out. The facility that also serves custom crush clients. They are very convenient to downtown Napa.

Elizabeth Spencer Wines – Tasting Room in Rutherford – Wines: Sauvignon Blanc, Chardonnay, Pinot Noir, Syrah, Cabernet Sauvignon – 1165 Rutherford Road Rutherford CA 94573 www.elizabethspencerwines.com – (707) 963–6067 – Hours: 10:00am – 6:00pm – The original Rutherford Post Office from 1872, across from BV. Recently purchased by Boisset.

Ellman Family – Collectors with a downtown tasting salon – Wines: Cabernet Sauvignon – 1461 First Street, Napa CA 94558 – www.ellmanfamilyvineyards.com – (707) 947–3010 – Hours: Appointment – Vineyards are near Reynolds.

Elyse Winery – Small & South of Yountville – Wines: Zinfandel, Cabernet Sauvignon, Petite Syrah, Syrah, Rhone Blends – 2100 Hoffman Lane Napa CA 94573 – www.elysewinery.com – (707) 944–2900 – Hours: 10:00am – 5:00pm Appointment.

Envy Wines – Near the Calistoga Geyser – Wines: Cabernet Sauvignon, Petite Syrah, Sauvignon Blanc – 1170 Tubbs Lane Calistoga CA 94515 www.envywine.com – (707) 942-4670 – Hours: 10:00am – 4:30pm Appointment – They are located down a curving drive just off Tubbs lane to the north of downtown Calistoga. They are relaxed and friendly with good wines. It is a pretty building in a convenient northern location.

Etude – Carneros Pinot – Wines: Pinot Noir, Merlot, Cabernet Sauvignon, Pinot Blanc, Pinot Gris – 1250 Cuttings Wharf Road Napa CA 94559 – www.etudewines.com – (707) 257-5300 – Hours: 10:00am – 4:30pm Appointment – This is a larger facility with interesting buildings and a European feel. They have been producing high quality Pinot Noir for many years and continue to do so. They do a bar tasting and a nice sit-down tasting of their more expensive wines.

Failla – Great Pinots North of Saint Helena – Wines: Pinot Noir, Viognier, Syrah, Chardonnay – 3530 Silverado Trail, Saint Helena CA 94574 – www.faillawines.com – (707) 963-0530 – Hours: 10:00am – 5:00pm Appointment – They make some of the best Pinot Noir in Napa because the grapes come from Sonoma's Coastal region, which has ideal conditions for that finicky grape. They have cool caves with the entire winery inside. They have a good staff that works both in a charming bungalow tasting room, and in the cave tasting. It is a seated tasting and you will be part of a small group. They are across the street from the Rombauer entrance, which is good to know since the Failla sign is not obvious, being small, and written on the mailbox.

Fairchild – Ultra Premium for Collectors – Wines: Cabernet Sauvignon – P.O. Box 2000, Saint Helena CA 94574 – www.fairchildwines.com – (707) 963-9990 – Hours: Appointment – members@fairchildwines.com – Their tastings are at a home in the Deer Park section on the slopes of Howell Mountain. These are serious wines that the owner pours for you.

Fairwinds Estate – Calistoga on the Silverado Trail – Note: Their tasting room and winery were destroyed in the 2020 Glass fire, wine club members can taste in the cave by appt. Map I

Fantesca Estate – Spring Mountain Collectors – Cabernet Blends – 2920 Spring Mountain Rd, St Helena, CA – www.fantesca.com – (707) 968-9229 – They are tucked a short way up Spring Mountain Road at the end of a long driveway. The winemaker is Heidi Barrett and it is owned by the founders of Best Buy. They have a home on the other side of the rise which can be reached through the straight through wine cave next to the simple winery. The views from the crush pad of the vineyards and the valley below are nice and the wines are first class. The tasting is in a conference room above the winery and the fees are a bit high, considering the low-key experience.

Falcor Winery – Corporate Park– Wines: Bordeaux Blends – 2511 Napa Corporate Drive, Napa CA 94558 –www.falcorwines.com – (707) 255–6070 – Hours: Appointments

Far Niente – A Great Estate – Wines: Cabernet Sauvignon, Chardonnay, Dolce, Sauterne style – 1350 Acacia Dr. Oakville CA 94558 – www.farniente.com – (707) 944–2861 – Hours: 10:00am – 4:00pm Monday–Saturday Appointment – This is an architectural jewel surrounded by wonderful grounds, ponds, fountains, cork oaks and event spaces. The tasting can include a tour of the winery and the car collection. They make wonderful world–class wines and do a sit–down tasting inside and in the gardens. When making your appointment take special care to determine which experience you want to do.

Farella Vineyards – Coombsville – Relaxed Family Winery
Wines: Sauvignon Blanc, Merlot, Cabernet Blanc, Blends – 2222 North Third Ave. Napa CA 94558 – www.farella.com – (707) 254–9489 – Hours: Appointment – This charming winery sits in the hills on the beautiful east side of Napa. The property is in its second generation and their knowledge of their vineyards shows in their wonderful wines. The tasting is relaxed, at home Napa, and on a completely different level from the 'stand at the bar' tasting most people are accustomed to. They vineyards were planted in 1977 by the father, Frank Farella, and they were the first Coombsville winery to produce a Cabernet Sauvignon. Son Tom Farella, the longtime wine maker. They were the authors of the petition to have Coombsville made an official American Viticulture Area, or AVA.

Faust – Perched on a Hill in St. Helena – Wines: Cabernet and other Bordeaux vareitals – 2867 St Helena Hwy, St Helena, CA 94574 – www.faustwines.com – (707) 200-2560 – Hours: Appointment – The main building was constructed in the late 1800's. Today it is connected with Quintessa and Russian River's Flowers, to feature Cabernet blends that come from their vineyard in Coombsville, a relatively cool AVA to the east of downtown Napa. The renovation turned it into a lovely, comfortable experience, with views of the valley and plenty of places to be sit. They are perched on a small hill just north of Beringer, and the building is painted a dark brown that makes it blend. There is a small winery facility onsite.

Favia Winegrowers – Coombsville Collectors – Wines: Bordeaux and Burgundy – P.O. Box 6978, Napa CA 94558 – www.faviawine.com – (707) 256-0875 – Hours: Appointment.

Fe Wines - Spring Mountain - Two Cabernet Blends - Saint Helena - www.fewines.com - 707-244-1191 - This is a newer winery with a small organic vineyard on the lower slopes of Spring Mountain, bordered by Bothe Park. The land was not previously farmed and the first grapes were harvested in 2016. They were made into the estate wines starting in 2018 by winemaker Aaron Potts, a local and respected consultant. They make two big pricey red blends. The property is rustic and charming and the name Fe comes from the scientific notation for Iron because the soil is high in that rugged mineral.

Fleury Winery – Unique – Wines: Bordeaux varietals – 950 Galleron Road, Rutherford CA 94574 – www.fleurywinery.com (707) 967–8333 – Hours: Appointment – This is a fun, high energy tasting room but watch out for large pours!

Flora Springs Winery – Tasting room – Wines: Cabernet Sauvignon, Sangiovese, Merlot, Rosato, Chardonnay, Pinot Grigio, Blends – 677 South St Helena Highway (Highway 29). Saint Helena CA 94574 – www.florasprings.com (866) 967–8032 Hours: 10:00am – 5:00pm Their Highway 29 tasting room is a modern, architecturally interesting place. It includes a reserve tasting room and two outdoor seating areas. It is across the street from V. Sattui next to a large market.

Foley Johnson– Rutherford Variety – 8350 St Helena Highway (Hwy 29). Rutherford CA 94573 – www.foleyjohnsonwines.com (707) 963–1980 – Hours: 10:00am – 5:00pm Appointment This little winery in Rutherford is part of the Foley Family Wine Group which owns an impressive portfolio of small, premium wineries. This winery is used as a sort of ambassador for the wine club that incorporates many of the labels.

Folie a Deux Winery - A Building Shared with Napa Cellars Wines: Blends, Zinfandel, Cabernet Sauvignon, Sangiovese, Syrah – 7481 St Helena Highway (Highway 29). Oakville CA 94562 – www.folieadeux. com – (707) 944-2565 – Hours: 10:00am–6:00pm Appointment –

They make good, well-priced wines with a steady following. The place is small, comfortable with a nice picnic area. Their location just north of Yountville near Cosentino makes them convenient. Their placement on the southbound side of the road, makes them convenient for a late in the day visit.

Fontanella Family Winery – Mount Veeder Family Winery – Wines: Chardonnay, Cabernet Sauvignon and Zinfandel – 1721 Partrick Road Napa CA 94558 – www.fontanellawinery.com – (707) 252-1017 – Hours: Appointment – A friendly family winery a bit of a ride up Mount Veeder, it comes with great views. They are a charming couple with years of experience, and they produce solid wines with lots of character.

Forman Vineyards – Small and Ultra-Premium – Wines: Cabernet Blend, Chardonnay. 1501 Big Rock Road Saint Helena CA 94574 – www.formanvineyard.net – (707) 963-3900 – Hours: Appointment – They are in their own canyon, down a steep road and they make wonderful wines. Ric Forman was Sterling's founding winemaker and he takes a hands-on, classical approach to his own label. Be on the lookout for signs as they are minimal.

Forthright Winery – Small for Collectors – Wines: Bordeaux & Burgundy – 2255 Dry Creek Road Napa, CA, 94558 Appointment – www.forthrightwinery.com – A small winery that sources grapes from their own small vineyard and others.

Fortunati Vineyards – A small family winery with good wines at reasonable prices – Wines: Bordeaux and Burgundy – 980 Salvador Ave, Napa, CA 94558 – www.fortunativineyards.com - (707) 255-9300 – Hours: 10:00am – 5:00pm Appointment – They are located just outside the city of Napa, but convenient from the downtown. The wines are nicely priced.

Frank Family Vineyards – Gracious and Fun Calistoga – Wines: Chardonnay, Sparkling, Cabernet Sauvignon, Zinfandel, Sangiovese 1091 Larkmead Lane Calistoga CA 94574 – www.frankfamilyvineyards.com – (707) 942-0859 – Hours: 10:00am – 5:00pm Appointment – The tasting is in a beautiful craftsman style mansion, with spacious rooms and surrounded by beautiful grounds. They are well-known for their humor and style. This is the site of the historic Larkmead Winery. They have a nice picnic area, and first-rate wines including a delicious sparkling wine in the rich and creamy Grand Cru style.

Freemark Abbey – Great Traditions – Wines: Chardonnay, Viognier, Merlot, Cabernet Sauvignon, Sauvignon Blanc, Zinfandel, Zinfandel Port, Petit Syrah, and Syrah – 3022 St Helena Highway (Highway 29) at Lodi Lane, Saint Helena CA 94574 – www.freemarkabbey.com – (800) 963–9694 – Hours: 10:00am – 5:00pm Appointment – The site first became a winery in 1886. The main building dates to 1899 when it was the Lombarda Cellars. They shipped a great deal of wine to the Italian stone masons in Barre, Vermont, the site of America's largest marble and granite quarries. It has passed through numerous owners and since 1966 has been owned by a group of families. They produce a wide variety of well–made wines. This is a charming winery with a nice outdoor patio and lots of seating plus a tasting bar. Freemark Abbey is a combination of the partner's last names.

Frias Family – In the City of Napa – Wines: Bordeaux and Burgundy – 1886 El Centro Ave, Napa 94558 – www.friasfamilyvineyard.com – (707)–927–5106 – Hours: 10 – 3 Monday–Sunday Appointment.

Frisinger Winery – Collectors Mount Veeder – Wines: Bordeaux and Burgundy – 3033 Dry Creek Rd, Napa, CA 94558 – www.frisinger-familywine.com – (707) 338–5009 – Hours: Appointment – This is a family vineyard that has been selling their grapes to other wineries for years, before returning to their original idea of making their own wines. So, the wines have a good history and an authentic story.

Frog's Leap Winery – Remarkable Organic Winery – Wines: Merlot, Zinfandel, Chardonnay, Sauvignon Blanc, Cabernet Sauvignon, Syrah, Blends – 8815 Conn Creek Road Rutherford CA 94558 – www.frogsleap.com – (800) 959–4704 – Hours: 10:00am – 4:00pm Appointment – This organic winery has a beautiful green hospitality center. They also taste on the patios, the garden and in the historic red barn. They make great wines; have a wonderful tour and a lovely staff. They have been organic growers for many years. The signs on the street are not big, so watch the numbers and look for the BIG red barn on the north side of the road. The tasting room is to the right.

Futo Estate – Western Oakville Hillsides – Big Cabernet Blends for Collectors – 1575 Oakville Grade, Oakville, CA 94562 – www.futoestate.com – (707) 944-9333 – This rather extraordinary winery is perched on a hill in the very pricey west side of Oakville. Coming from Hwy 29 it is accessed by the first road to the left past the Far Niente driveway. They are located between Promontory and Bond, and the wines are on the same elevated level, so the wines are expensive.

Gamble Family Vineyards – Ultra–Premium for Collectors – Wines: Bordeaux, Burgundy Blends – 7554 Saint Helena Highway, Yountville CA 94559 – www.gamblefamilyvineyards.com (707) 944–2999 – The hospitality space is just off Highway 29 near Cardinale. The buildings are spare, white farm architecture and the focus is the wines, not the place or the architecture. The vineyards, which are in sight, extend all the way east to the Silverado Trail. These are big, impressive wines.

Gandona Estate – Ultra–Premium Mountain Vineyards - Wines: Bordeaux Blends 1533 Sage Canyon Rd, St Helena, CA 94574 – www.gandona.com – (707) 967-5550 .

Gargiulo Vineyards – Oakville Charm for Collectors - Wines: Bordeaux Blends – 575 Oakville Cross Rd Napa CA 94558 – www.gargiulovineyards.com – (707) 944–2770 – Hours: 10:30am – 3:30pm Appointment – This is a charming private winery with great views of Napa's best vineyards. They spent three years re–engineering their land before planting their grapes. The Gargiulo family has a long tradition with agriculture, and they know how to make a great bottle of wine. They do a relaxed, elegant seated tasting at specific times with a knowledgeable staff. This part of the valley is home to some of Napa's most prestigious wineries; Silver Oak, Rudd, Groth, Vine Cliff, Harlan, Cardinale and Far Niente.

Gemstone – Collectors just north of the Yountville Cross Road on the Silverado Trail – Wines: Bordeaux and Burgundy Blends P.O. Box 3477, Yountville CA 94559 – www.gemstonewine.com – (707) 944–0944 – This is a simple tasting in a home, with a space to host guests and vineyards outside.

Ghost Block – Oakville, Previously the Napa Wine Company – Bordeaux and Burgundy, General French – 7830–40 Highway 29, Oakville CA – www.ghostblockwine.com – (707) 944–1710 Hours:10:00am – 3:30pm Appointment – the Perlissa family has been farming Napa for over a hundred years. Their family, the Hoxseys, run the Napa Wine Company which is an important custom crush facility. They converted their group tasting room into a private tasting room for their Ghost Block Wines and their other family labels.

Girard Winery – Calistoga – 1077 Dunaweal Lane, Calistoga, CA 94515 – Wines: Cabernet Sauvignon, Cabernet Franc, Petite Syrah, Zinfandel, Chardonnay, Sauvignon Blanc www.girardwinery.com – 707–234–4151 – Hours: 10:00am – 5:00pm Appointment – This is a well-respected label that is now owned by a group that manages numerous wineries. The Calistoga property is the winery facility and it features a spacious tasting area that looks out at the vines.

Girard Downtown Yountville Tasting Room – 6795 Washington Street Yountville CA 94599 www.girardwinery.com – (707) 968–9297 – Hours: 10:00 – 6:00.

Godspeed Vineyards – Mount Veeder Fruit – Chardonnay, Cabernet Sauvignon, Malbec, Blends – 3655 Mt. Veeder Road Napa Ca 94559 707–254–7766 – Hours: Appointment – A small estate winery producing three reasonably priced wines. Navigation Tip: To get to the winery take the Oakville Grade to the intersection of Mount Veeder Road, and then south to the vineyards. Do not drive north from Redwood Road, the drive is very curvy and slow. Not shown on our maps.

Goosecross Cellars – Yountville Charm – Wines: Bordeaux and Burgundy – 1119 State Lane Yountville CA 94599 – www.goosecross.com – (707) 944–1986 – Hours: 10:00am – 4:30pm Appointment – This small winery went through a major transformation to create a new facility and tasting room with outdoor patio tasting areas and great views. The wine list and the staff are wonderful. Near downtown Yountville.

Green and Red – A Unique Experience in Eastern Napa – 3208 Chiles Pope Valley Road Saint Helena, CA 94574 – www.greenandred.com (707)–965–2346 – Hours: Appointment – This is a winery for the adventurous, in Chiles Valley. The family started farming their hillside vineyards in the 1970's and have sold their grapes to excellent wineries. Their own wines are reasonably priced, and the story is wonderful. The name comes from the red chert and the green serpentine in the soil of their vineyards. It is currently in the second generation.

Grgich Hills Cellar – Judgment of Paris Wine Maker – Wines: Chardonnay, Fumé Blanc, Violetta, Cabernet Sauvignon, Zinfandel, Merlot 1829 St Helena Highway South(Highway 29) Rutherford CA – www.grgich.com – (707) 963–2784 – Hours: 9:30am – 4:30pm – Tours – Grgich Hills has a great reputation and what they lack in 'pretty', they make up for with friendly, quality and value. The windowless tasting room was recently the barrel room. Mike Grgich (Pronounced 'gur gitch'), from Croatia, worked with Beaulieu Vineyard's revered winemaker Andre Tchelistcheff. Later he was the winemaker at Chateau Montelena when they produced their top ranked Chardonnay at the 1976 Judgment of Paris that put Napa on the wine map. Grgich Hills Winery (named for the Hills Bros. coffee family that is the other partner) was born on July 4th. 1977. They have Biodynamic vineyards that are managed by Mike's nephew and the winery is managed by his daughter. The tasting room staff is knowledgeable and relaxed. This is a Wine Train stop.

Groth Vineyards – Big Pink – Wines: Cabernet Sauvignon, Chardonnay, Sauvignon Blanc – 750 Oakville Cross Road Oakville CA 94562 – www.grothvineyards.com – (707) 754–4254 – Hours: 10:00am – 4:00pm Appointment – This is a grand building in pink stucco with good wines and a beautiful tasting space. This is quintessential Oakville, so they range from Premium to Ultra-Premium.

Haber Family – Collectors – Wines: Bordeaux and Burgundy 345 Pine Breeze Drive Angwin CA 94508 –www.haberfamilyvineyards.com – (707) 965–9177 – Hours: Appointment - A small Howell Mountain family winery.

Hagafen Cellars – Oak Knoll Kosher Wines – Wines: Riesling, Syrah, Cabernet Franc – 4160 Silverado Trail Napa CA 94558 – www.hagafen.com – (707) 252–0781 – Hours: 10:00am – 5:00pm – Technically Oak Knoll AVA is across the road, but they share the qualities of this unique area. This is a nice, open air tasting room with kosher wines that have been served at the White House. The owner was one of Domaine Chandon's first employees. He has run Hagafen Cellars, which is the Hebrew word for wine, for many years for a devoted clientele.

Hall Wines – Wine and Sculpture – Wines: Cabernet Sauvignon, Merlot, Sauvignon Blanc – 401 St Helena Highway South (Hwy 29). Saint Helena CA 94574 – They have a second location off Rutherford Road called the Katherine Hall winery that can visited by Appointment – www.hallwines.com – (707) 967–2626 – Hours: 10:00am – 5:30pm. This larger winery is across from Louis M Martini, and it is a modern Architectural design that doubles as an exhibition space for the owner's art collection, including the giant bunny at the front of the property leaping through the vines, that you cannot miss. The floor to ceiling windows in the main tasting room are cool. They make good wines and have a pleasant staff. For the enthusiast, visit their beautiful mountain top Katherine Hall winery caves. This is a more expensive visit, but the views are great, and the sit–down tasting is in one Napa's most beautiful caves. It is lined with antique bricks from Austria and the hallways feature smaller pieces from their sculpture collection.

Hans Fahden Vineyards – Mountain Location. This winery is most popular as an event space. – Wines: Cabernet Sauvignon 4855 Petrified Forest Rd Calistoga CA 94515 – www.hansfahden.com – (707) 942-6760 – Hours: Appointment.

Harlan Estate – High End Collector Trophy Wines – Cabernet Blends – www.HarlanEstate.com – At a $1000.00 a bottle by allocation they don't need to be in the directory, but people ask where they are located so…! Their other label Bond is located nearby.

HdV - Hyde de Villaine Wines – Trancas Street Convenient – Wines: Chardonnay, Pinot Noir, Syrah, Cabernet Blend – 588 Trancas Street, Napa 94558 – www.hdvwines.com – (707) 251-9121– Hours 10:am – 5:00pm Appointment – This little winery on Trancas Street is a partnership of two families connected by marriage. Their central themes are Pinot and Chardonnay. The vines are in Los Carneros and on Sonoma Mountain.

Heitz Wine Cellars – Well Respected Label – Wines: Cabernet Sauvignon, Chardonnay, Grignolino, Rosé, Zinfandel, Port 436 St Helena Highway (Highway 29). South Saint Helena CA 94574 – www.heitzcellar.com – (707) 963-3542 – Hours: 11:00am – 4:30pm Appointment – This recently redone tasting room is conveniently located just south of downtown Saint Helena. Heitz is one of Napa's most respected names. Their wines have a great history, and the vineyards and home ranch where they also host guests are in a canyon off the Silverado Trail next to the Joseph Phelps winery. The tasting room is on the site of the original winery. It changed hands and the new owners performed a complete transformation of the site.

Hendry Wines – Northern Edge of Carneros – Wines: Albariño, Pinot Gris, Chardonnay, Rosé, Pinot Noir, Primitivo, Blends, Zinfandel, Cabernet Sauvignon – 3104 Redwood Road Napa CA 94558 – www.hendrywines.com – (707) 226-8320 – Hours: Appointment with Tour – The property has been in the family since the 1930's and there have been vineyards there since the 1860's. They do a great tour of the vineyards. You should plan on spending two hours. It is in an area with only a few other wineries. Navigation Tip: It is 2.5 miles from Highway 29 on the way to the Hess Collection.

Hess Persson Estates – Art Collection on Mount Veeder – Wines: A wide variety, Olive Oil, Vinegar – 4411 Redwood Road Napa 94558 – www.hesspersonestates.com – (707) 255-1144 – Hours: 10:00am

– 5:30pm – This destination winery houses a world class modern art collection on several floors of an historic stone barn, facing another barn that houses a state–of–the–art winery. The tasting room and gift shop are worth seeing by themselves. The barns are classic historic Napa and owned by the Christian Brothers Winery who have their center next door. Hess is located on Mount Veeder in the southwest corner of Napa, north of Carneros. The ride there on Redwood road is winding. The outstanding art collection makes the ride very much worth the effort.

Hestan Vineyards – Downtown Yountville with Cookware
Wines: Bordeaux and Burgundy – 6548 Washington Street Yountville CA 94559 – www.hestanvineyards.com – (707) 945–1002 – Hours: 11:00am – 6:00pm – This tasting room doubles as a showroom for this family's well known cookware.

Hill Family Estate – Downtown Tasting Room – Wines: Chardonnay, Pinot Noir, Merlot, Cabernet Sauvignon, Syrah – 6512 Washington Street, Yountville CA 94599 – www.hillfamilyestate.com – (707) 944–9580 – Hours: 10:00am – 6:00pm – Their tasting room is in the center of Yountville, but do not let the location hide the fact that this is a winery with a great deal of depth. They own numerous vineyards around Napa and have been selling grapes to top wineries for many years. Besides the fun tasting in town, they also host tastings at a nearby property on Solano Ave. These are wonderful, authentic folks.

Holman Cellars – Corporate Park – 918 Enterprise Way G, Napa, CA 94558 – www.holmancellars.com – (707) 287–7557 Hours: Appt.

Honig Cellars – Charming Outside Tasting – Wines: Sauvignon Blanc, Cabernet Sauvignon – 850 Rutherford Road Rutherford CA 94573 www.honigcellars.com – (707) 963–5618 – Hours: 10:00am – 4:00pm Appointment – Their tasting patio is relaxed and stylish, and the mood is entertaining and gracious. They also do a more private, reserve tasting inside at a conference table. It is a serious look at their library wines, and it gives you a chance to realize that they own some very good vineyards in Rutherford. This is a family business in their third generation and the younger generation still brings a lot of enthusiasm to the game.

Hoopes Vineyards – Coombsville – Wines: Bordeaux and Burgundy 6204 Washington Street, Yountville CA 94559 –
www.hoopesvineyard.com – (707) 944–1869 – Appointment.

Hope and Grace Winery - Downtown Yountville - Interesting Single Varietal wines including Bordeaux and Burgundy styles, including Malbec, Lagrein, Petite Verdot - 6540 Washington Street, Yountville, California, 94559 - www.hopeandgracewines.com - (707)-944-2500 - This was one of Yountville's first tasting rooms and longevity speaks volumes about the quality of the wines and the unique selection that they offer. The charming space sits in the middle of the shopping area and it is well worth the visit. The winemaker has a long history in this area and that is obvious in where they source their fruit.

Hope and Grace Winery - Downtown Yountville - Interesting Single Varietal wines including Bordeaux and Burgundy styles, including Malbec, Lagrein, Petite Verdot - 6540 Washington Street, Yountville, California, 94559 - www.hopeandgracewines.com - (707)-944-2500 - This was one of Yountville's first tasting rooms and longevity speaks volumes about the quality of the wines and the unique selection that they offer. The charming space sits in the middle of the shopping area and it is well worth the visit. The winemaker has a long history in this area and that is obvious in where they source their fruit.

Hourglass – Calistoga Collectors – Wines: Bordeaux and Burgundy – 4208 Silverado Trail N, Calistoga, CA 94515 – www.hourglasswines.com – (707) 968–9332 – Hours: 10:00am – 4:00 pm Appointment – This is a beautiful little cave winery on the east side of the Silverado Trail in the north part of the valley. The wines are priced for collectors.

Hudson Vineyards – Wines: Bordeaux and Burgundy Blends 5398 Carneros Highway, Napa CA 94558 – www.hudsonvineyards.com – (707)–255–1455 – Hours: Appointment – This is a remarkable estate winery owned by long time growers on the north side of the Carneros Highway. They make a wonderful variety of wines that go beyond the supposed limits of this cool region. Look for the five flag poles. When bud break appears, or harvest begins, they run up the Jolly Roger, to show that they are an independent, and not a corporate property like many of their Carneros neighbors.

Hunter Glenn Estate – Multi-Generation Family Winery South of Yountville – Wines: Bordeaux and Burgundy Blends – www.hunterglenn.com – Hours: Appointment – Caroline@hunterglenn.com – The brother and sister team that grow the grapes, make the wine and market it bottle by bottle are the fourth generation on the lovely vineyards, tucked against the Mayacamas mountains. This property is a mix of hills and benchland and it produces wonderful wines. On the same property the brothers and sisters of the next older generation make a wonderful Cabernet Sauvignon blend under the Shifflett label.

Hunnicutt – Calistoga Collectors – Wines: Bordeaux, Burgundy 3524 Silverado Trail North, Saint Helena CA 94574 – www.hunnicuttwines.com – (707) 963–2911 – Hours: 10:00am – 3:30pm Appointment – They are located in a cave north of Saint Helena across from Rombauer. Several other wineries use the same cave complex.

Hyde Estate – Carneros – Wines: Burgundy – 1044 Los Carneros Ave, Napa CA 94558 – www.hydevineyards.com – (707) 265–7626 – Hours: 10:00am – 4:00pm Appointment – Long time Los Carneros grower who finally made their own wines. You can see their building from Carneros Highway.

Inglenook– Formerly Rubicon Estate and before that Niebaum Coppola and before that Inglenook, meaning a safe place – Napa Italian Style with History owned by the Coppolas – Wines: Chardonnay, Cabernet Sauvignon, Merlot, Cabernet Franc, Syrah, Blanc de Blanc, Rosé, Sauvignon Blanc, Pinot Noir, Zinfandel, Rubicon – 1991 St Helena Highway (Highway 29). Rutherford 94573 www.inglenook.com – (707) 968-1161 Hours: 10:00am – 5:00pm Appointment – Tours – This is the premier winery of the family of the movie director Francis Ford Coppola and his wife Eleanor, where they produce their best estate wines. It includes a spacious tasting room, an elegant gift shop and an espresso bar, which is a wonderful place to relax amid a day of tasting with some chocolate or a cigar, which they sell in the cafe. You can sail a boat in the fountain making this among the most family-friendly wineries in Napa. The staff is excellent and the whole feeling is gracious and special. It was the center of the Niebaum Estate that Francis gradually reassembled. 'Rubicon' comes from the story of Julius Caesar returning from Gaul after his victories there. His enemies rigged the laws against him so crossing the Rubicon River into Italy would make him a rebel. Once he crossed, there was no going back. Once Francis made his first wine there was no going back.

Italics Winegrowers – Coombsville Cave – Wines: Bordeaux and Burgundy, Blends – 70 Rapp Lane, Napa CA 94558 – www.italicswinegrowers.com – (707) 258–0106 – Hours: 10:00am – 3:30pm Appointment Monday – Saturday – This is a high end winery inside a spacious cave, surrounded by their vineyards.

J Gregory – City of Napa – Wines: Bordeaux and Burgundy – 1819 El Centro Ave, Napa CA 94558 – www.jgregorywines.com (707) 474–2149 – Hours: 10:00am – 4:00pm Appointment – Tasting room.

J Moss – Corporate Park – Wines: Bordeaux and Burgundy, General French – 901 Enterprise Way, Suite B, Napa 94558 – www.jmosswines.com – (707) 647–3388 – Appointment

JaM Cellars - Downtown Napa next to the Andaz Hotel - 1460 1st St, Napa, CA 94559 - jamcellars.com - (707) 265-7577 - JaM is a big brand and a force in the downtown, as owners of two local theaters. They also have a tasting among the vineyards in an old church building on Thompson Road in Los Caneros.

James Cole Estate Winery – Small Oak Knoll District – Wines: Chardonnay, Malbec, Cabernet Sauvignon – 5014 Silverado Trail Napa CA 94558 – www.jamescolewinery.com - 707) 251–9905 Hours: 10:00am – 5:00pm Appointment – They are located at the intersection of the Silverado Trail and Oak Knoll Road, owned by a local family. The tasting is casual, the staff friendly and knowledgeable, and the wines good. The building and tasting room are elegant and understated. When the Highway 29 wineries are busy, you might find a nicer experience here, away from the crowds.

Jarvis Vineyards – Remarkable Cave Winery – Wines: Chardonnay, Cabernet Sauvignon and Bordeaux varietals – 2970 Monticello Road Napa CA 94558 – www.jarviswines.com – (800) 255–5280 – Hours: 11am – 4:30 Appointment with tour The winery is inside their beautiful cave and tasting there is a unique experience, as you cross over a stream that runs through the caves so bring a sweater. They have an event space filled with museum quality crystals. On the drive watch for an outcropping that looks like a man smoking a pipe.

Jericho Canyon - Calistoga - 3322 Old Lawley Toll Rd, Calistoga, CA 94515 - www.jerichocanyonvineyard.com - (707) 942-9665 - This family owned and operated winery is tucked against the eastern palisades off the Silverago Trail just outside downtown Calistoga. They make Cabernet, Sauvignon Blanc and a Rose. A very pretty estate that is tucked away so allow extra time to get there.

Jessup Cellars – Downtown Yountville Tasting Room – Wines: Chardonnay, Rosé, Merlot, Zinfandel, Cabernet Sauvignon, Blends, Petite Syrah, Zinfandel Port – 6740 Washington Street Yountville CA 94599

– www.jessupcellars.com – (707) 944–8523 – Hours: 10:00am – 6:pm – They are popular with small tour companies so their tasting room can get filled up fast, but it is still fun. Some wonderful wines and the space doubles as an art gallery.

John Anthony Vineyards – Downtown Napa – Wines: Bordeaux and Burgundy – 1440 First Street, Napa CA 94558 – www.johnanthonyvineyards.com – (707) 265–7711 – Hours: 10am-8pm. They also offer vineyard tastings in their 'church'.

Joseph Cellars – Calistoga – Wines: Bordeaux – 4455 St Helena Highway Calistoga CA 94515 – www.josephcellars.com – (707) 942–999 – Hours: 10:00am – 4:30pm Appointment – This is a small winery with their cave behind them on Highway 29 just south of downtown Calistoga.

Joseph Phelps Vineyards – Beautiful Secluded Valley – Wines: Cabernet Sauvignon, Sauvignon Blanc, Syrah, Viognier, Dessert Wine – 200 Taplin Road Saint Helena CA 94574 – www.jpvwines.com – (707) 967–3720 – Hours: Appointment – They are in a gorgeous valley off the Silverado Trail. They offer seminars. They were the first Napa winery to create a Bordeaux–style blend. Navigation Tip: Taplin Road is on the east side of the Silverado Trail north of the intersection with Zinfandel Lane. It is a tight turn and the road is narrow so take your time.

Judd's Hill Winery – Custom Crush – Wines: Cabernet Sauvignon, Petite Syrah, Chardonnay, Merlot, Zinfandel, Pinot Noir 2332 Silverado Trail Napa CA 94558 – www.juddshill.com - (707) 255–2332 – Hours: 10:00am – 5:00pm Appointment - They pour their own wines, but they are also a custom facility. Unlike many that exist throughout wine country they work with clients as small as one barrel, which is tempting. They are near the corner of the Silverado Trail and Trancas Street.

Kelham Vineyards and Winery – True Napa – Wines: Cabernet Sauvignon, Sauvignon Blanc, Merlot, Chardonnay, Port - 360 Zinfandel Lane Saint Helena CA 94574 – www.kelhamvineyards.com – (707) 963–2000 – Hours: Appointment – This is a gracious, charming family run winery. They do seated tastings outside on a remarkable patio. They also taste inside where there is a unique art collection centered on wine labels. The tasting is done by the family, including the two winemakers. They are unusual because they allow the wines to age for many years before they release them, to produce the most spectacular results. This is not a tasting you want to rush. In 2021 they introduced an innovative multi-media wine and food pairing that is a remarkable experience people will remember fondly for years. They have beautiful architecture and gardens.

Kelleher Family Vineyard – At the Brix Restaurant – Wines: Bordeaux and Burgundy – PO Box 111 Oakville, Ca 94562 – www.kelleherwines.com – 866 531–2580 – Hours: Appointment This family owns Yountville's Brix Restaurant, their vineyards are beyond the back patio overlooking the valley floor. They pour at the edge of the vineyards and there is a bonus. You can arrange for your lunch, or a paring to accompany the tasting. Do not worry, the tables have umbrellas to protect you from Napa's abundant sunshine.

Kelly Fleming Winery – Calistoga – Wines: Bordeaux and Burgundy P.O. Box 1207, Calistoga CA 94515 – www.kellyflemingwines.com – (707) 942–6849 – Hours: 10:00 am – 3:00pm Monday–Saturday Appointment – Located down a long county road off the Silverado Trail, this Tuscan style winery is set against a hillside, with a long tunnel bored into the native rock. Kelly Fleming likes having a team of mostly women winemakers and they produce a lovely product.

Keenan Vineyards – Spring Mountain – Cabernet Blends and a variety of other grapes – 3660 Spring Mountain Rd, St Helena, CA 94574 – www.keenanwinery.com – (707) 963-9177 – They are located halfway up Spring Mountain Road, and down a long driveway. The winery building was constructed in the 1800's and from the comfortable and casual tasting room there are views of the vineyards. The wines are good and the hospitality down to earth and knowledgeable. This is family owned and the long-time owner is hands on. Plan extra time for the ride because you don't want to have to rush in the final parts the narrow drive.

Keever Winery – A small Yountville family winery with great views – Wines: Bordeaux and Burgundy Blends – P.O. Bo 2906, Yountville, CA 94559 www.keevervineyards.com – (707) 944–0910 – Hours: 11:00am – 2:30pm Appointment – A lovely hillside winery surrounded by vineyards south of Yountville. They are a small production, high-quality winery run by the family.

Kenzo Estate – Remarkable Cave Winery – Wines: Bordeaux & Burgundy – 3200 Monticello Road Napa CA 94558 – www.kenzoestate.com – (707) 815-6736 – Hours: Appointment – This is a beautiful estate in the eastern hills of southeast Napa. It was once the Olympic equestrian center before it was bought by Mr. Kenzo, a Japanese Billionaire, so it still has horse trails. It is an elegant winery building and cave complex with solid, well made wines.

Kenefick Ranch Vineyard & Winery – A small family winery just south of downtown Calistoga at the base of the eastern palisades – Wines: Sauvignon Blanc, Cabernet Franc, Grenache Blanc, Petite Sirah – 2200 Pickett Rd, Calistoga, CA 94515s – www.kenefickranch.com – (707) 942-6175 – Hours: Appointment – This is a famiy run business combining the first and second generations. They do interesting varietals.

K Laz Wines – Downtown Yountville Wine Retail Outlet and Tasting lounge – Wines: Bordeaux and Burgundy Blends, General French – 6484 Washington St Suite C, Yountville, CA 94599 –www.klazwinecollection.com – (707) 415–5040 – Hours: 10:00am – 5:00pm

Krupp Brothers Estate – two locations: Estate winery & Oxbow tasting room – Wines: Cabernet Sauvignon, Chardonnay- The Estate Address: 1094 Hardman Ave, Napa, CA 94558 – www.kruppbrothers.com – (707) 225–2276 – Hours: Appointment They taste at their lovely Tuscan style estate just north of the city of Napa. Although there are vineyards on the site, many of their best grapes come from the Stagecoach Vineyards high up on Atlas Peak, that the brothers developed in the 1990's. Even though they sold the Stagecoach vineyards to Gallo.

Kuleto Estate Family Vineyards – Top of Sage Canyon – Wines: Cabernet Sauvignon, Sangiovese, Syrah, Pinot Noir, Chardonnay – 2470 Sage Canyon Road Saint Helena CA 94574 – www.kuletoestate.com – (707) 963–9750 – Hours: Appointment – It is a long ride out Sage Canyon Road to the gate. The winding driveway up has 12 convex mirrors at the hairpin turns. The location is cool with the vineyards perched on top of the mountains and the buildings are unique, with a great mix of muscularity and grace.

La Sirena – The Wines of Heidi Peterson Barrett for Collectors Wines: An eclectic collection with a Cabernet at its core – PO Box 441, Calistoga CA 94515 – www.lasirenawine.com – (707) 942–1105 Hours: Appointment – They taste at the winery in Calistoga.

Ladera Vineyards – Calistoga – Wines: Bordeaux and Burgundy– 3942 Silverado Trail North Calistoga, CA 94515 (707) 965-2445 www.

laderavineyards.com – (707) 968–9900 – Their previous winery was sold to Cade and renamed Vineyard 13. But the label endures, and the wines are being made at the Brasswood custom crush facility, and they do their tastings there. They also do seated tastings at their location on the Silverado Trail just south of Larkmead Road. However, that site requires climbing many steps.

Lail Vineyards – Collectors – Wines: Bordeaux and Burgundy – PO Box 249, Rutherford, CA 94573 – www.lailvineyards.com – (707) 968–9900 – Hours: Appointment.

Laird Family Estate – Oak Knoll Copper Pyramid – Wines: Pinot Grigio, Chardonnay, Syrah, Cabernet Sauvignon, Merlot 5055 Solano Ave. Napa CA 94558 – www.lairdfamilyestate.com (707) 257–0360 Hours: 10:00am – 5:00pm Appointment
This pyramid building with a surrounding patio sits in Oak Knoll AVA, but the Laird family owns vineyards in various parts of Napa. The highly active winery you see through the window is their custom crush facility that serves numerous other wineries. The Laird family has a long history in Napa.

Laura Michael Wines – Previously called Zahtila, same owners Wines: Cabernet Sauvignon, Zinfandel, Chardonnay – 2250 Lake County Highway, Calistoga CA 94515 – www.lauramichaelwines.com – (707) 942–9251 – 10:00am – 5:00pm Appointment – This small, charming outisde downtown Calistoga makes nice wines and pours them with that friendly inclusiveness that makes Calistoga shine. The name comes from first names of the two owners.

Larkmead Vineyards – Calistoga Ultra–Premium – Wines: Cabernet Sauvignon, Merlot, Sauvignon Blanc – 1100 Larkmead Lane Calistoga CA 94515 – www.larkmead.com – (707) 942–0167 – Hours: 10:00am – 4:00pm Appointment – This white winery is easy to spot as you travel north on Highway 29 above Saint Helena. They are a quality producer and the family, which has long ties in San Francisco, has owned the vineyards for many years. They do a lovely seated tasting in their salon–like tasting room with great views of the vineyards.

Lava Vine – Tasting Room – Wines: Chardonnay, Cabernet Sauvignon, Syrah – 965 Silverado Trail Calistoga CA 94515 – www.lavavine.com – (707) 942–9500 – Hours: 10:00am – 5:00pm Their little tasting room is five minutes from downtown Calistoga. It gets its name because its vineyards are located on an old lava flow. Much of the northern valley was volcanic three to four million years ago, and that rocky soil is one of the elements that make the area so good for the Bordeaux–style wines.

Leto Cellars – Corporate Park – Wines: Bordeaux, Burgundy 759 Technology Way, Napa CA 94558 – www.letocellars.com – (707) 259-5386 – Hours: Appointment at 10:30am, 1:00pm, 3:30pm.

Lewis Cellars – Oak Knoll Collectors – Wines: Bordeaux and Burgundy – 4101 Big Ranch Rd, Napa CA 94558 – www.lewiscellars.com – (707) 255-3400 – Hours: 10:30am – 1:30pm Monday – Friday Appointment – The wines are respected and priced accordingly, although the tasting is understated.

Lokoya – Spring Mountain Premium Cabernet Sauvignon – 3787 Spring Mountain Road Saint Helena CA 94574 – www.lokoya.com – (707) 948-1968 – Hours: Appointment – This is an extraordinary building with a story, built many years ago from stone by a hermit winemaker, that is worth the ride by itself. The the Jackson family did a dramatic renovation to reflect the ultra-premium nature of the wines.

Long Meadow Ranch – Tasting Room at the Farmstead Restaurant Wines: Cabernet Sauvignon, Sauvignon Blanc, Sangiovese, Ranch House Red, Olive Oil, Beef Jerky. 738 Main Street St Helena CA 94574 – www.longmeadowranch.com – (707) 963-4555 – Hours: 11:00am–6:00pm The main property is a large-acre hillside farm, ranch and winery, producing not only wine and olive oil, but also produce and meats.

Louis M. Martini Winery – Great Wines in Central Napa – Wines: Cabernet Sauvignon, Zinfandel, Chardonnay, Merlot, Cabernet Franc, Syrah, Petite Syrah – 254 St Helena Highway South (Highway 29). Saint Helena 94574 (800) 321–9463 - www.louismartini.com – Hours: 10:00am – 6:00pm – Appointment – This winery started just after Prohibition ended, and then in the third generation it was sold to their long time family friends the Gallos who poured big money into this site. They produced a destination winery, with spacious tasting bars, gorgeous reserve room and an expansive tasting garden. The wines have always been good, and they are centrally located. The building includes spaces for large groups.

Macauley Vineyard – Downtown Saint Helena Tasting Room for Big Oakville Cabernets – Wines: Burgundy, Outliers – 1309 Main Street,

Saint Helena 94574 –www.macauleyvineyard.com (707) 963–1863 Hours: Appointment – In the 2nd generation.

Madonna Estate – Carneros – Wines: Pinot Grigio, Chardonnay, Pinot Noir, Merlot, Dolcetto, Cabernet Sauvignon, Riesling, Gewürztraminer, Muscat Canelli – 5400 Old Sonoma Road Napa CA 94559 www.madonnaestate.com – (707) 255–8864 – Hours: 10:00am – 5:00pm – This is an organic family winery with some dry farmed vineyards, which is unusual. They have a picnic area just off the road. They are convenient from San Francisco which makes them a popular tour bus stop. They are 3rd and 4th generation Italian American winemakers, and they make remarkably good wines that are properly priced. If there is no tour bus in their lot they are worth a visit.

Madrigal Family – Calistoga – Wines: Bordeaux & Burgundy – 3718 North Saint Helena Highway, Calistoga CA 94515 – www.madrigalfamilywinery.com – (707) 942–1065 – Hours: 10:00am – 4:00pm Monday–Sunday Appointment – These long time farmers from the northern part of the valley have a lovely tasting area attached to their small winery with views of the vineyards. They make some interesting wines.

Mahoney Vineyards – Los Carneros – Wines: Chardonnay, Pinot Noir – 1134 Dealy Lane, Napa CA 94558 – www.carneroswinecompany.com – (707) 253–9464 – Hours: Appointment – They are long time Los Carneros growers.

Maldonado Vineyards – Downtown Calistoga – Wines: Bordeaux, Burgundy, Syrah, Pinot Gris, Dessert – 1307 Lincoln Ave, Calistoga, CA 94515 – www.maldonadovineyards.com – (707) 942–1376 – Hours: 11:00am – 5:30pm – These folks produce great wines at a proper price. It have been long time fixtures in downtown Calistoga and they have a big and loyal following. It is very much a Mexican descended farming family business.

Marita's Vineyard – Small Coombsville Collectors – Wines: Bordeaux – PO Box 4164, Napa CA 94558 – www.maritasvineyard.com – (707) 259–5313 – Hours: Appointment – This is a very small producer of excellent wines from the hills of southeastern Napa. The vines are tended by the winemakers and they produce lovely flavors with great depth.

Markham Vineyards – Rock and Roll – Wines: Merlot, Cabernet Sauvignon, Sauvignon Blanc, Chardonnay – 2812 St Helena Highway North (Highway 29) Saint Helena CA 94574 – www.markhamvineyards.com – (707) 963–5292 – Hours: 11:00am – 5:00pm Appointment – This winery is located north of downtown Saint Helena. It is a well-known producer of middle of the road wines. They have a spacious tasting room with an art gallery featuring photography of Rock and Roll icons from the 60's and 70's, a nice gift shop and some good, well-priced wines. Their staff is always pleasant, and the grounds and patio are a pleasant place to hang out.

Maroon Winery – Small Family Coombsville – Wines: Bordeaux, Zinfandel – 3565 Hagen Road Napa, CA 94558 – www.maroonwines.com (707) 257–3040 – Hours: Appt – The drive at the NV Country Club.

Marston Family – Spring Mountain Collectors – Wines: Bordeaux , Burgundy – Saint Helena CA 94574 – www.marstonfamilyvineyard.com – (707) 963–8490 – Hours: Appt.

Martin Estate – Collectors – Wines: Cabernet Sauvignon Blends
Post Office Box 390 Rutherford, CA 94573 – www.martinestate.com (707) 967–0400 – The winery is on Conn Creek Road in Rutherford across from Frog's Leap. It sits behind trees in a long stone building that dates to the founding of the Beaulieu Winery in the late 1800's, for which this was originally constructed. But BV outgrew it in a couple of years. It served as a residence until the current owners restored it, built a winery on the ground floor and planted the small area along the side of the Conn Creek with vines.

Materra / Cunat – Oak Knoll – Wines: Bordeaux and Burgundy – 4326 Big Ranch Road, Napa CA 94558 – www.materrawines.com (707) 224–4900 – Hours: 10:00am – 4:30pm - This sits on the corner of Big Ranch Road and Oak Knoll Cross Road in an area known for being able to grow everything. This is a new winery and part of the facility serves custom clients. The wines are well made.

Matthiasson Winery – A wide variety of nicely priced wines west of downtown Napa –3175 Dry Creek Rd. Napa, CA 94558 – www.matthiasson.com – (707) 637–4877 – This is a real working winery, and the tastings are often outside in area next to the building. There is nothing fancy about the place, but they make highly respected, solidly good wine from multiple varietals at a reasonable price compared to many in Napa. The staff is casual and knowledgeable and fun to work with.

Maxville Lake – Chiles Valley – Wines: Bordeaux and Petite Syrah – 4105 Chiles Pope Valley Rd, Saint Helena CA 94574 –

www.maxvillelakewines.com – (707) 965–9378 – Hours: 10:00am – 4:00 pm Appointment – This is a very modern winery on a thousand acres in this Chiles Valley in the hills of eastern Napa. Vines have been planted there since the early 1970's and the new owner has invested in a new winery and hospitality center that overlooks their lake. They have an excellent wine making team.

Mayacamas – Ultra Premium Tasted in Downtown Napa or at the Estate – Wines: Bordeaux and Burgundy – Downtown 1256 First Street Napa, CA 94559 – Estate 1155 Lokoya Road, Napa CA 94558 – www.mayacamas.com – (707) 224–4030 – Hours: Downtown 11am-6m (Check Website) – In 2017 their historic winery building in the Mayacamas mountains burned down. They have rebuilt and tasting are possible at the estate, although it is much less convenient than the downtown location.

McKenzie-Mueller Vineyards & Winery – Los Carneros Family – Wines: Pinot Noir, Chardonnay – 2530 Las Amigas Rd, Napa, CA 94559 – www.mckenziemueller.com – (707) 252-0186 Hours: Appointment – These native Napans have been involved in wine making for more than fifty years. They produce 2000 cases yearly of authentic Los Carneros wines.

Melka Estates – Collectors Saint Helena – Wines: Bordeaux and Burgundy, General French – P.O. Box 509 Saint Helena, CA 94574 – www.melkaestates.com – (707) 963–6008 – Hours: Appointment – Philippe Melka is a prominent consulting winemaker and the winery is located at the intersection of the Silverado Trail and Deer Park Rd.

Mending Wall – Wines: Bordeaux and Burgundy Blends, General French – 3730 Silverado Trail N, St Helena, CA 94574 – www.mendingwall.com – (707) 709–4200 – Hours: 10:00am – 3:00pm Appointment – This custom crush facility and tasting room features the wines of the senior wine maker, Thomas Rivers Brown. It is a stylish tasting room with stellar wines.

Merryvale Vineyards – Downtown Winery – Wines: Sauvignon Blanc, Chardonnay, Merlot, Cabernet Sauvignon, Fortified Dessert Wine, Zinfandel, Pinot Noir – 1000 Main Street Saint Helena CA 94574 – www.merryvale.com – (707) 963–7777 – Hours: 10:00am – 6:30pm Appointment – The building was once owned by the Mondavi family during the days of bulk winemaking. It sits beside the railroad tracks, and they would pull tanker cars up to the barrel room and fill them up.

Now that grand room, lined with old wooden tanks is used for events, with a banquet table running the length of it. They have a big tasting bar, that is open late compared to their neighbors. The tasting room is adjacent to the winery's tank room and you can see the line of stainless tanks through the doorway. They are on the south edge of downtown Saint Helena and next to the restaurants Pizzeria Tra Vigne and Gott's Roadside. The wines are first rate, and they are popular.

Merus Wines – Premium Tucked in the Hills – Wines: Bordeaux and Burgundy – 424 Crystal Springs Road Saint Helena, CA 94574 – www.meruswines.com – (707) 251–5551 – Hours: 10:00am – 4:00pm Monday– Sunday Appointment –

Mia Carta Tasting Room - Downtown Napa - 1209 1st St, Napa, CA 94559 - www.miacartanapa.com - (707) 346-2244 - This is an excellent group tasting room across from the Archer Hotel featuring some of the valleys best from very small producers.

Migration Winery – Los Carneros – Wines: Chardonnay, Pinot Noir 1451 Stanly Lane Napa, CA 94559 – (707) 415-2298 – www.migrationwines.com – Hours: 10:00am – 3:30pm Appointment – This is a larger facility connected with Duckhorn, thus the 'fowl' reference. It is tucked off by itself, although you can see it from Highway 29. It is next door to the site of a new Stanly Ranch hotel.

Miner Family Vineyards – Great Views – Wines: Chardonnay, Viognier, Sauvignon Blanc, Cabernet Sauvignon, Pinot Noir, Merlot, Syrah, Zinfandel, Sangiovese, Rosato. 7850 Silverado Trail Oakville CA 94558 – www.minerwines.com – (707) 944–9500 Hours: 11:00am to 5:00pm – This is a fun winery with an interesting list made from grapes they source both inside and outside Napa. They have great views from the front patio and a friendly staff. You can see the entire winery from the tasting room and they have a cave for events.

Mira – Yountville – Cabernet Blends – 6170 Washington St, Napa, CA 94558 – www.miranapa.com – (707) 945-0881 – This is a new winery south of downtown Yountville new Bell Cellars. You can see the stone buildings on the east side of Highway 29 abeam of Wappo Hill. They harken back to the early stone wineries constructed in Napa in the late 1800's because the angles are based the Golden Mean. Similar angles were frequently used in the early buildings because they shed the rain and snow so well. Of course, Napa doesn't see snow on the valley floor, but the early builders and masons came from places where snow was an annual event. Even though they are a new winery their tasting fees are up there with the rest of Napa. The team is experienced, and the grapes are from good vineyards.

Mi Sueno Winery – Corporate Tasting Room – Wines: Bordeaux and Burgundy – 910 Enterprise Way Suite M Napa, CA 94558 – www.misuenowinery.com – (707) 258-6358 – Hours: 9:00am – 5:00 pm Monday–Saturday Appointment – The name means 'my dream'.

Monticello Cellars – Corely Family in Oak Knoll – Wines: Bordeaux and Burgundy – 4242 Big Ranch Road Napa CA 94558 – www.CorleyFamilyNapaValley.com – (707) 253-2802 – Hours: 10:00am – 4:30pm They are in the southern part of the valley just north of Downtown Napa, in the Oak Knoll district, nearby Materra and Trefethen. They are also the site of a scaled replica of the home of Thomas Jefferson, Monticello, although the bar tastings are done in a facing building, they do a high end tasting in the cellar under the Monticello replica building. They have a nice picnic area so reserve your table.

Morlet Family Vineyards – Collectors – Wines: Bordeaux and Burgundy – 2825 St Helena Highway, St Helena, CA 94574 – www.morletwines.com – (707) 967-8690 – Hours: Appointment – Owned by a couple. They make remarkable wines in their 1880 stone building just north of Saint Helena.

Mumm Napa – Sparkling Wines and Great Photo Gallery – Wines: Sparkling and Still Wines. 8445 Silverado Trail Rutherford 94573 – www.mummnapa.com – (707) 967-7700 – Hours: 10:00am – 5:00pm Appointment – This fun winery pours interesting sparkling wines inside their tasting room and outside on their expansive patio, with great views and a central location. They have a fantastic photography museum, with rotating exhibits and they offer tours. Even though most of their vineyards are to the south in Los Carneros, the founding winemaker chose this site for its beauty and reminded everyone that he had trucks to move the grapes.

Napa Cellars – Friendly Winery – Wines: Chardonnay, Sauvignon Blanc, Zinfandel, Cabernet Sauvignon, Merlot, Pinot Noir, Syrah. Picnic tables – 7481 Saint Helena Highway, Hwy 29 Oakville CA 94562 – www.NapaCellars.com – (707) 944-2565 - Hours: 10:00am – 6:00pm – They share the tasting room with Folie a Deux in an easy location just north of Yountville and they are open to 6 pm. They enjoy a loyal clientele and that makes the place a lot of fun.

Neal Family Vineyards – Howell Mountain – Wines: Cabernet Sauvignon, Sauvignon Blanc, Petite Syrah, Zinfandel – 716 Liparita Road Angwin CA 94508 – www.nealvineyards.com – (707) 965–2800 – Hours: 10:00am – 5:00pm Appointment - This is a small production, high quality, state of the art winery. They are a little bit of a drive up the mountainous winding roads, but if you are an enthusiast then it is worth it. Like many small wineries, they offer a tour.

Neyers Vineyards – Up a Winding Road – Wines: Bordeaux and Burgundy – 2153 Sage Canyon Road, Saint Helena 94574 www.neyersvineyards.com – (707) 963–8840 – Hours: 10:00am – 5:00pm Tuesday–Saturday Appointment – This small family winery is tucked up the narrow canyon that was hit by fires in 2017, but it has recovered well.

Newton Vineyard – *Note: The 2020 Glass Fire heavily damaged their buildings and gardens. Check their website* – Spring Mountain outside downtown St. Helena – Wines: Chardonnay, Merlot, Cabernet Sauvignon, Cabernet Franc, Petit Verdot – 2555 Madrona Ave. Saint Helena CA 94574 – www.newtonvineyard.com   (707) 963–9000 Hours: Appointment.

Nichelini Winery – Chiles Valley – Wines: Sauvignon Blanc, Chardonnay, Zinfandel, Petite Syrah, Cabernet Sauvignon, Primitivo – 2950 Sage Canyon Rd Saint Helena CA 94574 – www.nicheliniwinery.com – (707) 963–0717 – Hours: 10:00am – 5:00pm Appointment – This is one of Napa's oldest family wineries perched on a hillside in the Chiles Valley (rhymes with tiles). It is a twenty–minute ride from the Silverado Trail They make wonderful wine in a great location. When you see where they are and realize that the original settlers did much of this work by hand, it is amazing. There are some interesting stories about how the family handled Prohibition. That area was hit by fires in 2020, but they were well prepared to save their property and escaped without damage.

Nickel and Nickel – Oakville Charm – Wines: Chardonnay, Cabernet Sauvignon, Merlot, Syrah, Zinfandel – 8164 St Helena Highway (Highway 29) Oakville CA 94558 – www.nickelandnickel.com – (707) 967–9600 – Hours: 10:00am – 3:00pm Appointment They have beautiful buildings and gardens, and a great tour and sit–down tasting of their single vineyard wines. They are associated with Far Niente. You should do the tour if you can. The winery sits across from the Robert Mondavi Winery and you can spot it from the horses grazing in front.

Neiman Cellars – Collectors – Napa – www.neimancellars.com (707) 322–7478 – Hours: Appointment – info@neimancellars.com – 600 cases of wine made by Drew Neiman.

Oakville Ranch – The Hills of Eastern Oakville – 7781 Silverado Trail, Napa, CA 94558 – www.oakvilleranch.com – (707) 944-9665 – Even though the address is on Silverado Trail, that is just where the private road begins that leads up the eastern slopes of the Vaca Mountains where several estates make their home. This beautiful, expansive, organic, solar powered, 370-acre property, a thousand feet above the valley floor, is a marvel of nature. The views of the valley are wonderful, and the wines are a great expression of Oakville. Amazingly they are not 'over the top' expensive and the visit includes an ATV tour of the property so wear practical shoes. Make your appointment in advance and allow yourself extra travel time.

Oakville Market – **The 1881 Napa Tasting Room** – This is next to the Market but owned by the same people – Wines: A variety of Napa's most famous wines avaiable by the taste or glass – 7856 St Helena Highway, Oakville – www.1881napa.com – (707) 944–8802 – Hours: Open to the public 7am - 6pm.

O'Brien Family Vineyard – South of Yountville – Wines: Chardonnay, Merlot, Bordeaux Blend called Seduction – 1200 Orchard Ave. Napa CA 94558 – www.obrienfamilyvineyard.com (707) 252–8463 – Hours: 10am – 5pm Tuesday–Sunday Appointment – This is a family winery on a beautiful property that is convenient to downtown Napa. They do a good tour, romantic and personal and a wine tasting sitting in signt of the vineyards. The winery equipment is right next to the tasting room. The wines are quite special, as are the people who make it. Their vineyards are Biodynamic/Organic.

Odette Estate – Pretty Winery in Stags Leap – Wines: Bordeaux and Burgundy – They are connected to Plumpjack and Cade. 5998 Silverado Trail Napa CA 94558 – www.OdetteEstate.com – (707) 224–7533 – Hours: 10:30 – 4:00pm – This was the former Steltzner property which was bought by the Plumpjack group. It was transformed into a very socially appealing space, elegant, spacious, with indoor and outdoor tastings, while looking out over the vineyards.

Olivia Brion Winery – Wines: Burgundy and Rose – www.oliviabrion.com – (707) 287–2870 – Hours: Appointment – A very small winery project with an interesting story.

One Hope Winery – Rutherford Winemaking as Philantropy – Wines: A variety of still & sparkling – www.onehopewine.com – 8305 St Helena Hwy, Napa, CA 94558 – Half their profits go to good causes but tastings are very limited.

Opus One Winery – An International Standard – Wines: Two Bordeaux style Blends – 7900 St Helena Highway (Highway 29). Oakville 94562 www.OpusOneWinery.com – (707) 944–9442 Hours: 10:00am – 4:00pm Appointment – Tour – Opus One is found on wine lists around the world and sure to impress any client that you are entertaining. This extraordinary building looks like an Incan temple, a white exterior submerged into green lawns surrounded by vines which are grown in the European method. The shape actually mimics a wine glass. It was started in the 1970's by the Baron von Rothschild and Robert Mondavi to combine European technology and California grapes. They produce one red wine made from the five Bordeaux varietals. Schedule tours well in advance.

Orin Swift Cellars –Downtown Tasting Room Saint Helena – Wines: Cabernet, Syrah. 1321 Main Street St Helena (Highway 29) CA 94574 www.orinswift.com – (707) 976–9179

O'Shaughnessy Estate Winery – Howell Mountain – Wines: Cabernet Sauvignon, Merlot. 1150 Friesen Dr Angwin CA 94508 www.oshaughnessywinery.com – (707) 965–2898 – Hours: Appointment – This is a beautiful, isolated winery started in 2000 with a unique curved cave. If you are an enthusiast, it is worth the drive. They email directions through the a maze of small roads.

Otra Vez Winery – Wines: Cabernet Sauvignon – 2280 Greenwood Ave, Calistoga CA 94515 – www.otravezwinery.com – (707) 942–4310 Hours: Appointment – This is a project by Vincent Arroyo, whose originally winery you pass on the way here. Very small production and high quality.

Outpost Wines – Howell Mountain – Wines: Zinfandel, Grenache, Petite Syrah, Cabernet Sauvignon. 2075 Summit Lake Dr. Angwin CA 94508 – www.outpostwines.com – (707) 965–1718 Hours: Appointment – On the top of Howell Mountain looking across at Spring Mountain. While they produce some wonderful wines, they are known just as much as a crush facility for some of Napa's hot labels. It is quite a ride to the top, but the views and the wines are great. Get them to send you directions.

Ovid – Collectors – Wines: Bordeaux Style – 255 Long Ranch Road, Saint Helena CA 94574 – www.ovidnapavalley.com – (707) 963–3850 – Hours: Appointment – This ultra-premium winery overlooks the Napa Valley. They are on the eastern ridge of the valley so allow extra time to get there up the narrow, winding road.

Palladian Estate Winery – Saint Helena – 690 Meadowood Lane St. Helena, CA 94574 – www.palladianwine.com – (707) 963–7106 – Hours: 10:00am – 4:30pm Monday – Friday Appointment – This is a rustic winery just outside Saint Helena next to the Meadowood Resort that makes good wines and pours them outside.

Palmaz Vineyards – Big Coombsville Caves – Wines: Cabernet Sauvignon Blends, Riesling, Chardonnay, Muscat Cannelli - 4029 Hagen Road Napa CA 94559 – www.palmazvineyards.com – (707) 226-5587 – This five story high cave winery is located to the east of downtown in an area that, thanks to its geology, has numerous cave wineries. The tasting area sits high on the hillside. Allow two hours for the tour and tasting.

Paoletti Vineyards – Italian Style – Wines: Bordeaux and Super Tuscan blends, Nero d' Avola (Sicilian varietal similar to a new world Shiraz), Rose of Sangiovese – 4501 Silverado Trail Calistoga CA 94515 – www.giannipaoletti.com – (707) 942–0689 - Hours: 10:00am–5:00pm Appointment – This is an Italian–style building with marble sculptures in their cave. The property sits at a curve on the Silverado Trail. They do a casual tasting for a group. They lean towards Italian varietals.

Paradigm Winery – Premium Oakville – Wines: Merlot, Cabernet Sauvignon, Zinfandel, Cabernet Franc – 683 Dwyer Road Oakville CA 94562 – www.paradigmwinery.com – (707) 944–1683 – Hours: Appointment – This is a well–respected winery just a short ride off Highway 29. The sign at the beginning of Dwyer Road says, "No Wineries this Road" but it is past their turn so do not believe everything you read!

Paraduxx – Pair of Ducks – Wines: Bordeaux Blends, Cabernet/Zinfandel, Rhone twist blend. 7257 Silverado Trail Yountville CA 94558 www.paraduxx.com – (707) 945–0890 – Hours: 11:00am–4:00pm by Appointment – This winery sits by itself just off the Silverado Trail north of the intersection with Yountville Cross Road. The name means 'a Pair of Ducks' because it was started by the Duckhorn family to feature their Cabernet/Zinfandel blend. They do a sit–down tasting with a food pairing with indoor and mostly outdoor seating.

Parallel Winery – Wines: Cabernet Sauvignon – 3125 Saint Helena Highway North (Highway 29) Saint Helena, CA 94574 – www.parallelwines.com – (707) 363–8600 – Hours: 10:00am – 6:00pm Appointment – Not open to public – Taste at the Vintner's Collective or at Brasswood Cellars.

Patland Estate Vineyards – Caves at Soda Canyon - Wines: Bordeaux and Burgundy – www.patlandvineyards.com – 888 539–4717 Hours: Appointment.

Peju Province Winery – A Rutherford Jewel – Wines: Sauvignon Blanc, Chardonnay, French Colombard, Syrah, Merlot, Cabernet Franc, Zinfandel, Cabernet Sauvignon, Blends – 8466 St Helena Highway (Highway 29) Rutherford CA 94558 – www.peju.com – (707) 963–3600 – Hours: 10:00am – 6:00pm – The grounds are sprinkled with sculptures and beautiful plantings. The building and rooms are elegant, and the gift shop is unique. The wines are well made and often sourced from Pope Valley. Our suggestion is to visit here early in the day.

Pestoni Family – Previously Called Rutherford Grove – Wines: Cabernet Sauvignon, Merlot, Sauvignon Blanc, Petite Syrah, Sangiovese – 1673 Saint Helena Highway Saint Helena CA 94574 – www.pestonifamily.com – (707) 963–0544 – Hours: 10:00am to 4:30pm Appointment – This family first arrived in Napa in the late 1800's. Their most popular wine is their Sauvignon Blanc. The winery is surrounded by their vineyards.

Piña Cellars – Hillside Winery – Wines: Cabernet Sauvignon, 5 Cabernets from 5 vineyards – 8060 Silverado Trail Rutherford CA 94573 – www.pinacellars.com – (707) 738–932 – Hours: 10:00am – 4:30pm This is a small winery with good wines. The family runs a long–time vineyard management company so they grow good grapes, some of which are on the hillsides just above the small winery. The tasting room is also the barrel room. This is a fun experience and the staff is knowledgeable and often involved in the winemaking process.

Phifer Pavitt – Collectors – Wines: Bordeaux – 4660 Silverado Trail Calistoga California 94515 –www.phiferpavittwine.com –
(707) 942–4787 – Hours: Appointment.

Pine Ridge Vineyards – Stags Leap District – Wines: Chenin Blanc/ Viognier Blend, Rosé, Merlot, Cabernet Franc, Malbec, Cabernet Sauvignon – 5901 Silverado Trail Napa CA 94558 – www.pineridgevineyards.com – (800) 575-9777 – Hours: 10:30am –4:30pm – This winery sits in its own pretty canyon convenient to many other good wineries. The grounds are lovely, although the best sections are reserved for the wine club members. The tasting room is spacious and connected to the barrel cave, which can be seen through the glass doors.

Plumpjack Winery – Small Winery Big Wines – Wines: Cabernet Sauvignon, Merlot, Chardonnay, Syrah. – 620 Oakville Cross Road Oakville 94558 – www.plumpjack.com – (707) 945-1220 – Hours: 10:00am – 4:00pm Appointment – This is just off Oakville Cross Road, by Silver Oak, B Cellars and Groth. Their sign is at the bottom of the hill. The narrow driveway goes through the vines to this small tasting room. The winery equipment is across the courtyard from the tasting room, so during the crush in late August through November there is a lot to see. The winery's name and emblematic signs have an old English theme related to Shakespeare and Queen Elizabeth.

Pope Valley Winery – A Long Ride – Wines: Chenin Blanc, Sangiovese, Sangiovese Rosé, Zinfandel, Merlot, Cabernet Sauvignon, Zinfandel Port – 6613 Pope Valley Road CA 94567 – www.popevalleywinery.com (707) 965-1246 – Hours: 11:00am – 5:00pm Thursday – Appointment – This is a small winery 30 minutes over the mountains from the valley floor in the Pope Valley. Many Napa wineries source grapes from this area. This winery dates from 1897. One warning: It gets hot in Pope Valley so save for a cooler day.

Porter Family Vineyards – East Napa Caves – Wines: Bordeaux and Burgundy, Syrah – 1189 Green Valley Road Napa, CA 94558 – www.porterfamilyvineyards.com – (707) 265-7980 – Hours: Appointment A beautiful winery in the eastern hills that does tastings in their cave which is underneath their vines.

Prager Winery and Port Works – Fun and Cozy – Wines: Late Harvest Riesling, Petit Syrah, Port – 1281 Lewelling Lane Saint Helena CA 94574 – www.pragerport.com – (707) 963-7678 – Hours: Monday-Saturday 10:30-4:30 Appointment – A cozy, eccentric tasting room run by a family with a loyal customer base. Tasting there is like enjoying a favorite port in your uncle's den papered with money. They are behind a large house out of sight of the road. Look for the sign by the driveway.

Pride Mountain Vineyards – Stunning Views – Wines: Merlot, Cabernet Sauvignon, Cabernet Franc, Viognier, Chardonnay – 4026 Spring Mountain Road Saint Helena CA 94574 – www.pridewines.com – (707) 963–4949 – Hours: Appointment – This beautiful winery sits on the top of Spring Mountain. The Napa Sonoma County line runs through their caves which you tour. They have a great picnic area available to customers. Allow 25 minutes for the steep, winding drive from downtown St Helena. The buildings and caves are neat, and they sell 'I survived my drive to Pride Mountain Tee shirts.

Prime Cellars – Coombsville Winery with Tasting Room in Downtown Napa – Wines: Bordeaux and Burgundy – 974 Franklin Street, Napa CA 94558 – www.primenapa.com – (707) 258–9773 – Hours: 12:00pm – 6:00pm.

The Prisoner – Former location of Franciscan – Wines: Bordeaux and Burgundy – www.theprisonerwinecompany.com – 1178 Galleron Rd, St Helena, Ca 94574 – Hours: 10:30am – 4:00pm Appointment – A black, steam punk gulag looking experience, complete with chains, manacles and wine. It can handle large groups in its many different rooms, including its expansive outdoor patio.

Progeny Winery – Mount Veeder Collectors, Views and Pairings – Wines: Bordeaux and Burgundy – 1032 Mt Veeder Rd, Napa CA 94558 www.progenywinery.com – (707) 252–9466 Hours: 9:00am – 5:00pm Appointment.

Promontory Winery – Ultra–Premium with Great Views – Wines: Big Cab Blends – 1601 Oakville Grade, Oakville CA 94547 www.promontory.wine (707) 944–0125 – Hours: 9:00am to 5:00pm Appointment – concierge@promontory.wine – This is part of the Harlan Group. The tasting is expensive, but the wines, location and the experience are exceptional.

Prime Solum Winery – Tasting Room – 1021 Atlas Peak Road, Napa – www.primesolum.com – (707) 226–8569 – Hours: 11:00am – 5:00pm – closed Tuesday and Wednesday.

Provenance Vineyards – The Big Red Building with a Mural Wines: Sauvignon Blanc, Merlot, Cabernet Sauvignon, NV Port 1695 St. Helena Highway (Highway 29) Saint Helena CA 94574 – www.provenancevineyards.com – (707) 968–3633 – Hours: 10:00am – 5:30 Appointment – This is a big spacious winery that makes some seriously good wines. They have a very social tasting room with an expansive tasting bar, a small gift area and a nice staff.

Quintessa – The Curving Wall – Wines: Bordeaux Blends – 1601 Silverado Trail Rutherford CA 94573 – www.quintessa.com – (707) 967–1601 – Hours: Appointment – This high–end winery focuses on one Bordeaux–style blend that they offer with a food pairing. The tasting/tour is wonderful, and the facility is beautiful. They are easy to spot of the Silverado Trail due to their remarkable building, built in a curve. The caves go directly into the hillside behind the building and the tasting room sits on top like a hat. They have a great staff and they are surrounded by their Biodynamic vineyards.

Quixote Winery – Most Unique Buildings – Wines: Cabernet Sauvignon, Grenache and Mourvèdre, Petite Syrah – 6126 Silverado Trail Napa CA 94558 – www.quixotewinery.com – (707) 944–2659 – Hours: Appointment – One of Napa's most unique winery buildings. They do a seated tasting that takes 1 to 2 hours for the tour and tasting. Many people come here just to see the building, which was the last project of an Austrian architect with a devoted following. The tile work is remarkable!

Rarecat Wines – Collectors – They are one of the wineries at Mia Carta in downtown Napa – Wines: Burgundy, General French, Outliers – www.rarecatwines.com – (707) 968–5031.

Raymond Vineyard – Zinfandel Lane – Wines: Cabernet Sauvignon, Merlot, Chardonnay, Sauvignon Blanc, Petite Syrah, Rosé, Meritage – 849 Zinfandel Lane Saint Helena CA 94574 - ww.raymondvineyards.com – (707) 963–3141 – Hours: 10:00am – 4:00pm – This is owned by Jean Charles Boisset of Burgundy and Napa and he has transformed it into a show piece with diverse educational opportunities and delightful experiences, including the valley's best educational Biodynamic gardens, that is home to goats and chickens. The winery is always changing as the owner invents new experiences and spaces for the visitors to enjoy. The Raymond family was part of the Beringer family, that established this winery after Beringer was sold. Boisset owns Buena Vista and DeLoach in Sonoma.

Razi Winery – Southern Silverado Trail – Wines: Bordeaux & Burgundy – 3106 Silverado Trail Napa CA 94558 – www.raziwinery.com – (707) 224–4299 – Hours: Monday–Saturday Appointment – A small winery with a yellow sign.

RD Winery – Asian Style Tasting Room – Wines: A Wide, Eclectic Variety – 3 Executive Way, Napa CA 94558 – www.rdwineryus.com – (707) 259-9446 – Hours: Monday–Saturday by Appointment – This was Napa's first Vietnamese owned winery. Originally the wines were made for export to Vietnam. They now produce a variety that are either sold through the beautifully designed tasting room or limited distribution. The winery facility was originally owned by a Japanese sake producer and it is large enough that it produces both their own wines while providing services for custom crush clients. They are located south of downtown Napa at a busy commercial intersection near the Napa airport. The site is part of a corporate park filled mostly with companies serving the wine industry. One of the coolest aspects of RD is the variety of wines that they make.

Realm Cellars – Stags Leap Collectors – Wines: Blends – 5795 Silverado Trail, Napa CA 94558 – www.realmcellars.com – (707) 224–1910 Hours: Appointment – For the serious collector. This was the location of the Hartwell Winery until they sold the site to their winemaker.

Regusci Winery – Stags Leap District – Wines: Cabernet Sauvignon, Merlot, Zinfandel, and Chardonnay. 5584 Silverado Trail Napa CA 94558 – www.regusciwinery.com – (707) 254–0403 – Hours: 10:00am – 5:00pm – Their stone barrel barn is the oldest winery building in the Stags Leap District. This is a working farm, because the Regusci family manages vineyards for numerous wineries. But they also make their own wine, that comes from the vineyards closest to the barn and tasting room. They have a good staff and a beautiful property. If you want to get the feeling of authentic Napa this is the place to come. They also make olive oil.

Reid Family Vineyards – Wines: Bordeaux and Burgundy
1020 Borrette Lane, Napa CA 94558 – www.reidfamilyvineyards.com – (707) 252–3195 – Hours: 10:00am – 4:00pm Appointment – reidfamily@reidfamilyvineyards.com – Sitting at the foot of Mt. Veeder, the estate was homesteaded in 1880 as a prune ranch and the original barn, where the tasting happens, remains. The Reids started in 1992, hand-crafting the wines using traditional barrel–to–barrel racking techniques without filtration or fining. They use French and American oak barrels and produce about 1000 cases of each year.

Relic Wine Cellars – Soda Canyon – Cabernet Sauvignon, Merlot, Syrah, Carignane – 2400 Soda Canyon Rd, Napa, CA 94558 – www.relicwines.com – (707) 967-9380 – They are located halfway up this narrow canyon that was devastated in the 2017 fire. Fortunately for the winemaker husband and wife team that own and operate it, the fires bypassed their site. Their winery is outside on a concrete pad two thirds of the way up the ridge, and the wine barrels are in the small cave. The view from the pad where tastings are often conducted are wonderful, as are the wines. Very much worth the ride. They are small so make your appointment well in advance. The grapes come from various vineyards.

Restoration Hardware – Also known as Ma(i)sonry – Collective Tasting Room and Design Center Downtown Yountville – 6711 Washington Street Yountville CA 94599 – www.maisonry.com – (707) 944-0889 – Hours: 10:00am–7:00pm – This is a combo of a tasting room for small production, high end wineries, a design center and restaurant. The seated tastings are by appointment, although if it is slow consider dropping by and asking for an instant appointment. The tasting is also a chance to see the furniture and design environment.

Revana Family Vineyard – Ultra Premium by Appointment – Wines: Cabernet Sauvignon, Merlot – 2930 St Helena Highway (Highway 29). North Saint Helena CA 94574 – www.revanawine.com – (707) 967-8814 – Hours: 10:00am – 4:00pm Appointment – This small winery is just off the road above Saint Helena. They have always employed name wine makers.

Reverie II Winery – Wines: Roussanne, Marsanne, Barbera, Tempranillo, Mountain Cuvee, Cabernet Franc, Cabernet Sauvignon – 264 N Fork Crystal Springs Rd, Deer Park, CA 94576 – www.reveriewine2.com – A charming, small family winery tucked in the hills and assciated with Aonair.

Reynolds Family Winery – Southern Silverado – Wines: Cabernet Sauvignon, Pinot Noir, Chardonna – 3266 Silverado Trail Napa CA 94558 – www.reynoldsfamilywinery.com – (707) 258-2558 – Hours: 10:30am – 4:30pm Appointment – It is a little surprising to find a winery that is this comfortable and relaxed, where the wines are so good, and convenient from downtown Napa. It is a nice combination, right off the Silverado Trail. They have a great side patio overlooking the pond. Their signature wine is called Persistences.

Rivers Marie Winery – Downtown Calistoga Winery – Wines: Cabernet Sauvignon, Pinot Noir, Chardonnay – 900 Foothill Blvd, Calistoga, CA 94515 – www.www.riversmarie.com – (707) 341-3127

– Hours: Appointment – It is the creation of Thomas Rivers Brown, a wine consultant, and his wife Genevieve Marie Welsh on the site of Marie's original family home.

Robert Biale Vineyards – Oak Knoll Zinfandels – Wines: Plus Petite Syrah, Barbera, and Sangiovese – 4038 Big Ranch Road Napa CA 94558 – www.robertbialevineyards.com – (707) 257–7555 – Hours: 10:00am – 5:00pm Appointment – This is another of those great Napa families that have growing good grapes for years. They make wonderful Zinfandels, and they offer them with that wonderful, relaxed Napa hospitality. The tasting room is small so most tastings take place outside on the comfortable patio.

Robert Foley Vineyards – Howell Mountain – Wines: Cabernet Sauvignon, Merlot, Syrah, Chardonnay – 1300 Summit Lake Dr, Angwin, CA 94508 – www.robertfoleyvineyards.com/ – (707) 965-2669 – Hours: They taste by appointment on Thursday, Friday & Saturday at 10:30am – 4:00pm Appointment

Robert Keenan Winery – Spring Mountain – Wines: Cabernet Sauvignon, Merlot, Zinfandel, Syrah, Chardonnay – 3660 Spring Mountain Road Saint Helena CA 94574 – www.keenanwinery.com – (707) 963–9177 – Hours: 11:00am – 4:00pm Appointment – This winery is about half the way up Spring Mountain. The drive narrow but pretty. The site had a winery on it before Prohibition and the owners did a beautiful job of restoring the building and providing vineyard views.

Robert Mondavi Winery – A Gracious Estate – Wines: Fumé Blanc, Chardonnay, Pinot Noir, Merlot, Cabernet Sauvignon, Moscato d'Oro, Dry Rosé – 7801 St Helena Highway (Highway 29) – Oakville 94558 – www.robertmondaviwinery.com – (707) 968–2001 – Hours: 10:00am – 5:00pm – Robert Mondavi was Napa's patron saint of marketing, a brilliant personality who was a tremendous influence the area's development. This big, California Mission style winery is almost a pilgrimage for many. It includes some of Napa's best vineyards, midway up the valley with the mountains towering above them. The spacious, rambling winery features sculptures, gardens, a gift shop, multiple tours, and a basic tasting room and the reserve To Kalon room, which is Greek for most beautiful or most high. That is where the big Cabernet Sauvignon wines are poured. These are available both in flights and individually. The winery is said to be on the less desirable western side of Highway 29, the thinking being that it was easier to catch inbound visitors on the eastern side of the road, but clearly, Robert

Mondavi overcame this perceived disadvantage. Today the winery is managed by Constellation Brands.

Robert Sinskey Vineyards – Stags Leap Biodynamic – Wines: Bordeaux, Burgundy, Zinfandel – 6320 Silverado Trail Napa CA 94558 – www.robertsinskey.com – (707) 944–9090 – Hours: 10:00am – 4:30pm Appointment with food pairings – This modern building sits above the road surrounded with lavender flowers and gardens on the Silverado Trail just south of Yountville Crossroad. It is a Biodynamic winery. When you enter the high vaulted space, you enjoy the aromas coming from the commercial kitchen in the back corner. One of the owners is a well-known chef and cookbook author and this winery has some of the best bar snacks in the valley. They have a delightful kitchen garden planted around the winery and a great patio with seating. Their caves are behind the winery and are used for special events. This is a fun place that draws a younger crowd.

Robinson Family Vineyards – Stags Leap District – Wines: Cabernet Sauvignon, Merlot – 5880 Silverado Trail Napa CA 94558 – www.robinsonfamilyvineyards.com – (707) 944–8004 - Hours: Appointment – This is a small, family winery down a country road with few signs. They don't seem to be currently hosting guests.

Rocca Family Vineyards – South Napa Tasting Room – Coombsville Wines: Bordeaux and Burgundy – 129 Devlin Road, Napa CA 94558 – www.roccawines.com – (707) 257–8467 – Hours: 10:00am – 4:30pm Monday–Saturday Appointment – Their hospitality center is a restored house built in the 1800's down the road from the Napa Airport. So, for those coming to Napa from San Francisco they are very convenient. The wines are from vineyards in Yountville and Coombsville.

Rombauer Vineyards – Hill Top Perch – Wines: Cabernet Sauvignon, Merlot, Chardonnay, Zinfandel, Port – 3522 Silverado Trail North Saint Helena CA 94574 – www.rombauervineyards.com (707) 963–5170 – Hours: 10:00am – 5:00pm Appointment – Their winery is perched on a hill, on top of a mile of narrow caves. Rombauer is a longtime favorite Chardonnay in restaurants. The family developed the winery while the father was an airline pilot and the mother managed another winery. They are part of the family connected to the book 'The Joy of Cooking'. At the Culinary Institute of America, a few minutes away, they display the many editions from the first, small and simple book.

Roots Run Deep – Downtown Napa Tasting Room – Wines: Bordeaux and Burgundy – 1607 First Street, Napa, California 94559 – www.rootsrundeep.com – (707) 254-8673 – Hours: 10:00am – 5:00pm They are connected to the Sunset Ranch Vineyards.

Round Pond Estate – Rutherford Dust and Olives – Wines: Cabernet Sauvignon, Nebbiolo and then some – 875 Rutherford Road Rutherford CA 94573 – www.roundpond.com – (707) 302-2575 – Hours: 11:00am – 4:00pm Appointment – This family owns hundreds of acres of vines in Rutherford, although most of the grapes are sold to other wineries. They also grow olives and their well-known press is across the way where they do olive tastings. The spectacular winery is at the end of a long palm tree lined drive was created for the small percentage of grapes that they hold onto for their own wines. The tasting room is beautiful with wonderful views of the valley. They also have a commercial kitchen and a tasting bar.

Rudd – Ultra-Premium and Beautiful – Wines: Cabernet Sauvignon, Chardonnay, Sauvignon Blanc, Blends – 500 Oakville Cross Road Oakville CA 94562 – www.ruddwines.com – (707) 944-8577 Extension 1 – Hours: Tuesday-Saturday Appointment – This is a winery for the collector. The tasting is expensive and so are the wines, but for the serious enthusiast it is a great experience. The gardens are lovely, and the winery is state of the art, even though the tasting is normally limited to the main building, there are extensive caves.

Rustridge Winery – Chiles Valley – Wines: Bordeaux and Burgundy – 2910 Lower Chiles Valley Road, Saint Helena CA 94574 www.rustridge.com – (707) 965-9353 – Hours: 10:00am – 4:00pm – It is a 25-minute ride from the valley floor to this far end of Chiles Valley (rhymes with miles). Back in the 1950's this was a horse ranch and now the main business is the winery. This area was hit by the Glass Fires in 2020 so check their website for updates and availability.

Rutherford Hill Winery – Great Views and Tour – Wines: Zinfandel Port, Merlot, Cabernet Sauvignon, Cabernet Franc, Sangiovese, Blends, Petite Verdot, Chardonnay, Syrah, Malbec, Sauvignon Blanc – 200 Rutherford Hill Road Rutherford CA 94558 – www.rutherfordhill.com – (707) 963-1871 – Hours: 10:00am – 5:00pm – They are on a hillside overlooking the valley with great views. They do an excellent tour and the wines are widely distributed. They have picnic tables under hundred-year-old olive trees with views of the valley available for a for a small fee. They also do some tastings there. They have nice indoor and outdoor tasting areas. Check their website for the tour schedule and then make an appointment. They are a popular winery for large corporate groups thanks to their expansive property and large caves.

Rutherford Ranch – Tucked Away – Wines: Cabernet Sauvignon, Chardonnay, Merlot, Sauvignon Blanc, Zinfandel, White Zinfandel, Port, Moscato – 1680 Silverado Trail Saint Helena CA 94574 – www.rutherfordranch.com – (707) 967-5120 – Hours: 10:00am – 4:30pm There are two wineries that start with 'Rutherford'. Even though it sits opposite the Conn Creek Winery, it cannot be seen from the Silverado Trail. The tasting room is bright and open. On the hills above is the hotel Auberge du Soleil and above that is the Rutherford Hill Winery.

Ru Vango– Los Carneros – 1285 Dealy Lane Napa CA 94559 – www.ru-vango.com – (707) 253-1615 – Hours: 11:00am – 5:00pm By Appointment – This modern design is fit into a traditional building near Artesa. The property was formerly Mahoney, then Michael Mondavi and Kieu Hoang. Their patio looks out at the vineyards and hills.

Saddleback Cellars – Rustic in Oakville – Wines: Pinot Blanc, Pinot Grigio, Chardonnay, Viognier, Merlot, Old Vine Zinfandel, Cabernet Sauvignon – 7802 Money Road Oakville CA 94562 – www.saddlebackcellars.com – (707) 944-1305 – Hours: 10:00am – 4:00pm Appointment – The winery is owned by Nils Venge, a well-respected consulting winemaker. It is a small winery on Money Road which is across from the entrance to Silver Oak Winery. Tastings are done outside on picnic tables next to the vines. It is surprising to find such a relaxed, natural winery tucked among all the heavy hitters of Oakville.

Saintsbury Vineyard – Carneros – Wines: Pinot Noir, Syrah, Chardonnay – 1500 Los Carneros Ave. Napa – www.saintsbury.com – (707) 252-0592 – Hours: Appointment – This long time partnership is widely respected for their Pinot Noir. It is a short distance off Carneros Highway, although not clearly marked so use the street signs and mailbox numbers. They taste at garden tables next to the winery and vineyards. In cold weather they move inside the winery.

Salvestrin Vineyard and Winery – Saint Helena – Wines: Cabernet Sauvignon, Sangiovese, Retaggio (Red Blend), Sauvignon Blanc, Petite Syrah – 397 Main Street Saint Helena CA 94574 – www.salvestrinwinery.com – (707) 963-5105 – Hours: Appointment

– This small family winery is just south of downtown Saint Helena. The tastings are private with nice views of the vineyards. They have been farming Napa since 1932 and released their first vintage in 1994. The wines are good and the experience is enjoyable.

Schramsberg Vineyards – Classic Sparkling Wine Cave Tour Wines: Sparkling Wines and Cabernet Sauvignon – 1400 Schramsberg Road Calistoga CA 94515 – www.schramsberg.com – (707) 942-4558 – Hours: 10:00am–4:00pm Appointment – This is an historic cave winery at the top of a long, winding road. Allow extra travel time and arrive early. The tasting includes the tour and they are set at specific times, so you do not want to be late. The Davies family restored the winery, producing world class sparkling wines in the process.

Schweiger Vineyards – Top of Spring Mountain – Wines: Sauvignon Blanc, Chardonnay, Merlot, Cabernet Sauvignon, Petite Syrah, Port – 4015 Spring Mountain Road Saint Helena CA 94574 – www.schweigervineyards.com – (707) 963-4882 – Hours: 11am – 4:00pm Appointment – This family-run winery is in a beautiful location at the top of Spring Mountain. They have great views and the tasting room sits on rise with great views of the vineyards and the valley beyond. The father grows the grapes, the son makes them into wine, and the daughter runs the tasting room. How cool is that?

Screaming Eagle – Eastern Oakville Cabernet Based Trophy Wine – www.screamingeagle.com – At $3000.00 plus a bottle with an annual production of less than a 1000 cases they don't need to be in the directory, but people ask where they are located so...!

Seavey Vineyard – Conn Valley – Wines: Cabernet Sauvignon, Merlot – 1310 Conn Valley Road Saint Helena 94574 – www.seaveyvineyard.com – (707) 963-8339 – Hours: 10:00am – 4:00pm Appointment – It is a fifteen-minute drive out Conn Valley to the winery. The stone dairy barn that now serves as the winery was built in 1881. The hills are planted with grapes. It is a beautiful place and a nice tasting.

Sequoia Grove Winery – Relaxed and Friendly – Wines: Cabernet Sauvignon, Chardonnay, Syrah – 8338 St Helena Highway (Highway 29). South Rutherford CA 94558 – www.sequoiagrove.com – (707) 944-2945 – Hours: 10:30 – 5:00pm Appointment – They are next to some of the area's most famous wineries and they can hold their own for quality. A charming, relaxed tasting room and a friendly staff. Look for the Sequoia trees next to the building as your landmark.

Seven Apart – Southern Silverado Trail – 4057 Silverado Trail, Napa, CA 94558 – www.sevenapart.com – (707) 287-1347 Appointment – The wine maker is Andy Erickson, a highly respected and long time member of the wine making community. They are focused on Cabernet. It is new in 2021 and is geared to collectors. However, it is very conveniently located near to the Soda Canyon store.

Seven Stones – Wines: Cabernet Sauvignon – 840 Meadowood Ln, St Helena, CA 94574 – www.sevenstoneswinery.com (707) 963–0993 – Hours Appointment – info@sevenstoneswinery.com – This is a unique property that serves in part as a site for the owners sculpture collection. The production is small.

Shafer Vineyards – Ultra Premium Stags Leap District Producer – Wines: Chardonnay, Cabernet, Blends – 6154 Silverado Trail Napa CA 94558 – www.shafervineyards.com – (707) 944–2877 – Hours: Tastings at 10am and 2pm Monday–Friday Appointment – Their Hillside Select is a world famous wine that comes from the beautiful canyon that you drive through on the way to the winery. As you drive north on Silverado Trail there is no sign, just a number. They have a lovely hospitality center perched on a rise that is spacious and light filled. They are one of Napa's great ultra–premium producers that recently changed hands. They have limited seats so plan well in advance.

Shadybrook Winery – Coombsville with Horses – Wines: Bordeaux and Burgundy – 100 Rapp Lane, Napa CA 94558 – www.shadybrookestate.com – (707) 254–9463 – Hours: 9:00am – 4:00pm Appointment – Charcuterie – In 2020 this was voted the best tasting room by the locals, with its spacious, comfortable patio and big pours. It is part of a property with commercial stables and trail rides through the vineyards.

Sherwin Family Vineyards – *Note: In the 2020 Glass fire their main building was destroyed, however their vineyards were fine, so we expect them to keep producing. Check their website for updates* – Spring Mountain – Wines: Cabernet Sauvignon, Blends – 4060 Spring Mountain Road Saint Helena CA 94574 www.sherwinfamilyvineyards.com – (707) 963–1154 – Hours: Appointment – Their vineyards sit at the top of Spring Mountain among other small wineries. Navigation Tip: They are located on the top of Spring Mountain. Take the road up the hill until you are on the top. After you pass the Schweiger winery on the right, look for a road going to the right and many mailboxes. There will also be winery signs. Turn right there and follow the signs for the number, 4060 and the winery name. This is the same drive that goes to the Barnett Winery.

Signorello Vineyards – Hillside Perch – Wines: Cabernet Sauvignon, Zinfandel, Pinot Noir, Syrah, Sauvignon Semillon Blend 4500 Silverado Trail Napa CA 94558 – www.signorellovineyards.com – (707) 255-5990 – Hours: 10:30am–5:00am Appointment – This is a charming, small family winery perched on the hillsides of Silverado just north of Darioush. They produce well–made wines from estate vineyards. They make a Sauvignon Blanc, Semillon blend. In 2021 they opened a new winery perched on the top of their hill.

Silver Oak Cellars – Big Popular Red Wines – Wines: Cabernet Sauvignon Blends – 915 Oakville Cross Road Oakville 94558 www.silveroak.com – (707) 944-8808 – Hours: 9am–5am – The winery building is constructed with antique blocks from an 1800's flour mill. The tasting room is spacious, the parking easy, and the buildings are easily seen from the Oakville Crossroad at the end of its long, tree–lined driveway. The wines are Cabernet blends from Napa Valley and Sonoma's Alexander Valley. They use American oak barrels, which gives the wine a stronger vanilla flavor.

Silverado Vineyards – Great Views in Stags Leap – Wines: Sauvignon Blanc, Chardonnay, Merlot, Sangiovese, Cabernet Sauvignon – 6121 Silverado Trail Napa 94558 – www.silveradovineyards.com – (707) 257-1770 – Hours: 10:30am–5pm – Silverado is romantic, with its California Mission style building, perched on a hill in the Stags Leap district, with gorgeous views over the vineyards from the patio, or from the comfortable tasting room. The wines are well made and properly priced. The staff is friendly and accustomed to visitors from all over the world. The drive up to the top of their hill seems steeper than it really is, but the convex mirrors allow you to see around the corners. Take your wine out on the patio and enjoy the view. There is something special about this place, with its collection of small, rounded hills that gathers the morning fog and holds it there as the Sun rises, sending rainbows through the vines.

Sinegal Estate – Wines: Bordeaux and Burgundy – 2125 Inglewood Ave Saint Helena, CA 94574 – www.sinegalestate.com – (707) 244-1187 – Hours: Appointment – The manor house and gardens go back many years, but the hospitality center is new that is designed encourage a social scene. It is tucked at the end of road at the foot of the Mayacamas mountains just south of Saint Helena.

Smith-Madrone – Spring Mountain Riesling – Wines: Cabernet Sauvignon, Chardonnay, Riesling – 4022 Spring Mountain Road Saint Helena CA 94574 – www.smithmadrone.com – (707) 963–2283 – Hours: Appointment – They did their first vintage in 1977. They are down home and relaxed.

Sodaro Estate Winery and Vineyard – Coombsville – Wines: Cabernet Sauvignon, Cabernet Franc, Blends – 24 Blue Oak Lane Napa CA 94558 – www.sodarowines.com – (707) 975–6689 – Hours: Appointment – This charming winery on the east side of Napa sits on a small hill and the tasting is on the patio over looking the valley.

Somnium Wine – Downtown Calistoga Tasting Room – Wines: Cabernet Sauvignon – PO Box 307, Saint Helena CA 94574 – www.somniumwine.com – Deer Park CA 94508 – (707) –287-2246 – Hours: Appointment. The vineyards of Danica Patrick are on the steep, rocky hillsides of Howell Mountain. The 24–acre estate property includes six organic planted acres of Cabernet Sauvignon, Cabernet Franc, and Petit Verdot. As of 2021 the property and winery were still under development, although they were already making wine.

Spelletich Family – Corporate Park Winery – Wines: Bordeaux and Burgundy – 2545 Napa Valley Corporate Dr, Suite C Napa, CA 94558 – www.spellwine.com – (707) 775–7300 – Hours: Appointment.

Spottswoode Winery – Downtown Saint Helena – Wines: Cabernet Sauvignon, Sauvignon Blanc, Blends – 1902 Madrona Ave. St. Helena CA 94574 – www.spottswoode.com – (707) 963–0134 – Hours: Appointment – This winery is at the edge of suburban St. Helena. The owner and winemaking team are almost all women. Their permit allows them limited visitors so book 6–8 weeks in advance for an appointment. This property has a lot of history, including their ghost winery from the 1800's, and the estate house and gardens, which are beautifully planted and part of the tour. They do small production.

Spring Mountain Vineyards – Classic Spring Mountain – Wines: Syrah, Cabernet Sauvignon, Sauvignon Blanc – 2805 Spring Mountain Road St. Helena CA 94574 – www.springmtn.com – (707) 967–4188 – Hours: 10:00am – 5:00pm This is a grand estate that has their wineries and mansion at the foot of Spring Mountain, and their vineyards stretch up the hillsides above them. They are one of the biggest vineyards on Spring Mountain, being a combination of several large properties. The mansion dates to the 1800's and it the house was used in the television series Falcon Crest. They taste beside the vineyards, in the caves or the mansion. While they were affected by the 2020 Glass fire, losing a house and outbuildings, the main areas and vineyards were untouched.

St Claire Brown – Downtown Napa – Wines: 850 Vallejo Street Napa, CA 94558 – www.stclairbrown.com – (707) 255-5591 – Hours: 12:00pm – 6:00pm – Check Website.

St. Helena Winery – Collectors – Wine: Bordeaux – 100 Pratt Avenue, Saint Helena, CA 94574 – www.sthelenawinery.com – (707) 967-9463 – Hours: 10:00am – 4:00pm Monday Saturday Appointment – This is an ultra-premium winery just off the Silverado Trail, but you are better off approaching it from Highway 29. It is a pretty Napa style ranch house.

St. Supéry Vineyards – Understated Elegance – Wines: Sauvignon Blanc, Cabernet Sauvignon, Merlot, Chardonnay, Unoaked Chardonnay, Syrah, Cabernet Franc – 8440 St Helena Highway (Highway 29). Rutherford CA 94558 – www.stsupery.com – (707) 963-4507 – Hours: 10:00am – 5:00pm Appointment – They are owned by Chanel and fronted by a beautiful Victorian house, but the tasting room and winery is modern. Many of the grapes are sourced from Pope Valley. Find a place at the bar away from the entrance.

Staglin Family Vineyard – Premium – Wines: Chardonnay, Cabernet Sauvignon, Sangiovese – 1570 Bella Oaks Lane Rutherford CA 94573 www.staglinfamily.com – (707) 963-3994 Hours: 11:00am – 3:00pm Monday–Friday Appointment – This is a well–respected family–run winery with stellar wines that is known for their architecture, their organic methods and philanthropic work. They have a large cave.

Stag's Leap Wine Cellars – The Judgment of Paris Winner – Wines: Sauvignon Blanc, Chardonnay, Merlot, Cabernet Sauvignon – 5766 Silverado Trail Napa 94558 – www.cask23.com (707) 261-6441 – Hours: 10:00am – 4:30pm Appointment The Stags Leap district is in the southeastern corner of the Napa Valley. It is also the name of two wineries separated by an apostrophe. Stag's Leap Wine Cellars is one of Napa's most famous wineries for its win in the Judgment of Paris wine tasting in 1976 when their Cabernet Blend took the top position. The original family sold it in 2008 to Antinori and Chateau St Michele. They constructed a very modern hospitality center next to the caves with wonderful views of their vineyards and the hillsides beyond including the Stags Leap Peak. They do cave tours and seated tastings by appointment and their cave tasting room can accommodate a large group, in case you are planning a corporate event. The wines are authentic Stags Leap Region.

Stags' Leap Winery – Petite Syrah – Wines: Viognier, Chardonnay, Merlot, Cabernet Sauvignon, Petite Syrah – 6150 Silverado Trail Napa CA 94558 – www.stagsleapwinery.com – (707) 944-1303 – Hours: Appointment – This winery has tons of history and stories back to the 1800's. They taste in the Ivy-covered Manor House, which has been featured in both television and movies. Plan on making your plans well in advance. Because of the similarity of their name with their neighbors, Stag's Leap Wine Cellars, people often become confused and call the wrong winery. It was their neighbor that won the Judgment of Paris for their Cabernet. However, this winery's approach is much different, and they are most known for their less traditional wines, especially their fantastic Petite Syrah. It is currently owned by Beringer.

Sterling Vineyards – Ride the Gondola to Wine and Views – Wines: Cabernet Sauvignon, Merlot, Chardonnay, Pinot Noir, Shiraz, Sauvignon Blanc, Blends – 1111 Dunaweal Lane Calistoga 94515 – www.sterlingvineyards.com – (707) 942-3344 Hours: 10:00am – 4:30pm This iconic winery south of Calistoga is famous for the aerial tramway that brings you to the mountain top tasting room. It is a fun time, with great views and a wide variety of wines. Allow at least two hours for your visit. As you travel north and pass Larkmead Lane you can see Sterling's bright white building perched on its hilltop. Note: The 2020 Glass Fire scorched the hillsides around Sterling and they have removed numerous trees.

Stony Hill Vineyard – Tucked Away – Wines: Chardonnay, Cabernet Franc – 3331 North St Helena Highway (Highway 29) Saint Helena CA 94574 – www.stonyhillvineyard.com – (707) 963-2636 – Hours: Appointment – This is a small winery up a long narrow road. Saying that it is on Highway 29 is not accurate. You enter via the drive to the Bale Grist Mill and then just before the park's entrance you take the drive to the left which goes to the winery. The property started off as a family home that became vineyards and a winery. The tasting may be a bit of ride, but it is well worth the time.

Storybook Mountain Winery – The Northern Edge – Wines: Zinfandel, Cabernet Sauvignon – 3835 Highway 128 Calistoga CA 94515 – www.storybookwines.com – (707) 942-5310 –Hours: Monday-

Saturday by Appointment – This is a beautiful location on the edge between the Napa Valley and Knight's Valley. The tour/tasting is normally done by the owners. It is a special place, although a bit of a ride. The tasting is done in the caverns dug into the hills in the 1800's.

Strala Vineyards – Premium Wines Tasted at Brasswood – Wines: Bordeaux and Burgundy Blends – 5 Financial Plaza, Napa, CA 94559 (707) 339–2244 – Hours: Appointment – www.stralavineyards.com – A family with deep connections in the grape growing and wine making that produce good wines well priced for the quality.

Sullivan Vineyards Winery – A Rambling Family Winery – Wines: Rosé, Chardonnay, Bordeaux Blend, Cabernet Sauvignon, Merlot – 1090 Galleron Road Saint Helena CA 94574 www.sullivanwine.com – (877) 244–7337 – Hours: 10:00am–5:00pm Appointment – They make big red wines and create a gracious tasting experience at their property behind the Prisoner Winery. The tasting room is elegant, and the outside patio is delightful. Off in the distance is a pond.

Summit Lake Vineyards and Winery – Howell Mountain – Wines: Cabernet Sauvignon, Zinfandel, Zinfandel Port – 2000 Summit Lake Dr. Angwin CA 94508 – www.summitlakevineyards.com – (707) 965–2488 – Hours: by Appointment - This is a small family winery about 20 minutes from the Silverado Trail. The tasting is at the home of the owners and the tasting is outside in the garden if weather permits. Their first commercial vintage was in 1978 and won gold medals. They do small production on site, and some wines are only available at the winery. For the quality, the prices are good.

Sutter Home Winery – Big Selling Brand – Wines: Variety of modestly priced wines – 277 St Helena Highway South (Highway 29). Saint Helena 94574 – www.sutterhome.com – (707) 963–3104 – Hours: 10:00am–5:00pm – This is one of Napa's biggest wineries, yet most of the grapes are brought in from other areas. They are known for their White Zinfandel, one of the biggest selling wines in America. The owners, the Trinchero family, own numerous wineries in Napa. It is a big, spacious tasting room with a friendly staff, a wide variety of wines and a nice gift shop. The tastings are modest, as is the price point. Many of their Zinfandel grapes come from Amador County, in the Sierra Madre foothills. That was gold rush country and viticulture was started there by miners who saw that as a good alternative to panning for gold. Their Amador county, deep red Zinfandel is their stand–out wine and a good deal. White Zinfandel is miss–named, being a pink wine, the reason being that the original wine was dry and white. It started off as a 'throw away juice', drawn off before fermentation so that the remainder would make a deeper, richer Zinfandel. One year they got sloppy and left some skins in the juice, and then the fermentation got stuck leaving some residual sugar. This pink, sweet accident was 'White Zinfandel'. They were stuck with the name and it has been a big seller ever since.

Swanson Vineyards – Transition – Wines: Merlot, Pinot Grigio, Rosato, Petite Syrah, Sangiovese, Syrah, Chardonnay, Blends, Muscat – www.swansonvineyards.com – Hours: Appointment The winery location was sold and the tastings are being done at Girard until they find a new one. Check the website.

Tamber Bey – Wine Making with Horses in Calistoga – Wines: Bordeaux, Burgundy – 1251 Tubbs Ln, Calistoga, CA 94515 – www.tamberbey.com – (707) 942–2100 – Built into an active stable and paddocks that are home to various horses. They have a wonderful pairing that shows off their wines. It is a unique experience. These were once called the Sun Dance Stables which were owned in part by Robert Redford, who had a home just down the Silverado Trail for many years. It was a covered riding rink because he preferred riding in the shade.

Taylor Family Vineyards – Stags Leap – Wines: Bordeaux – P.O. Box 2576, Napa CA 94558 – www.taylorfamilyvineyards.com – (707) 255–3593 – Hours: 10:00am – 5:00pm Monday Friday by Appointment – This lovely property sits in the heart of the famous Stags Leap District. The family personally planted the steep hillside vineyards and continue to make the wine. They typically pour on their patio that overlooks the valley. The wines are seriously good. They are located just south of the Silverado Vineyards, there is no sign, look for the number.

Taplin Cellars – Collectors – St Helena – Wines: Bordeaux and Burgundy – 1677 Lewelling Ln, St Helena, CA 94574 – www.taplincellars.com – (707) 968–9418 – Hours: Appointment – The Taplin family's history in Napa goes back to the 1800's. The vineyards are on the valley floor at the foot of the Mayacamas Mountains. It is family run and completely authentic.

Teachworth – Collectors – Wines: Bordeaux – 4451 Saint Helena Highway, Calistoga CA 94515 – www.teachworthcabs.com (707) 942–8432 – Hours: 10:00am – 4:00pm Appointment – Guest House Available for members – In the hills south of downtown Calistoga.

Tedeschi – Calistoga Relaxed – Wines: Bordeaux, Burgundy 2779 Grant Street, Calistoga CA 94515 – www.tedeschifamilywinery.com – (707) 501–0668 – Hours: 10:00am – 5:00pm Appointment This little family winery produces a wonderful array of good quality wines at reasonable prices inside the Calistoga city limits. It is run by the multi-generation family and it is surrounded by their vineyards.

The Crane Assembly – Collectors Historic Old Vines in Southern Saint Helena – Wines: Bordeaux and Burgundy – PO Box 989, Saint Helena CA 94574 – www.thecraneassembly.com – (707) 302–0989 – Hours: Appointment.

The Terraces – Adventurous – Wines: Zinfandel, Cabernet Sauvignon, Balsamic vinegar – 1450 Silverado Trail, Rutherford CA 94574 – www.terraceswine.com – (707) 963–1707 – Hours: 10:00am – 4:30pm Thursday–Sunday Appointment – They do their tour of this beautiful property in a 4–wheel drive. They have some of the few Zinfandel vines left in that section of Napa. They also make Balsamic vinegar.

The Wine Foundry – South Napa Industrial Park – Wines: – 45 Enterprise Ct STE 3, Napa Ca 94558 – www.thewinefoundry.com – Hours: 8:30am – 5:30pm Monday–Friday –Appointment – A custom crush facility that hosts various wineries.

Theorem Vineyards – Premium Calistoga – Wines: Bordeaux and Burgundy Blends – 255 Petrified Forest Road, Calistoga CA 94515 – www.theoremvineyards.com – (707) 942–4254 - On the site of the Graeser Winery. It was purchased a wealthy couple who transformed into a luxury winery.

Titus – Silverado Trail – Wines: Bordeaux and Burgundy – 2971 Silverado Trail, Saint Helena CA 94574 – www.titusvineyards.com – (707) 963–3235 – This winery sits on the west side of the Silverado Trail north of downtown Saint Helena, surrounded by their vineyards. They are long time growers who produce a solid wine and pour it on their lovely patio in site of the vines.

Tofanelli Family Vineyards – Calistoga Family Established 1929 – Wines: Charbono, Grenache, Petite Syrah, Zinfandel – 1212 Pine Street, Calistoga CA 94515 – www.tofanelliwine.com (707) 942–6504 – 10:00am to 4:30pm Appointment – They produce small lots of traditional grape varietals that were once widely planted in Napa Valley. The wine is made by the family and reasonably priced.

Tom Eddy Winery – Calistoga Tiny – Wines: Bordeaux & Burgundy – 3870 CA–128, Calistoga, CA 94515 – www.tomeddywinery.com – (707) 942–4267 – Hours: 10:00am – 4:00pm Appointment – This family winery is far up the valley. The office tasting room is simple, but the walk to the caves is part of what makes this special, as well as the excellent wines.

Tom Scott – Collectors – Wine: Cabernet Sauvignon – 1465 Yountville Cross Rd, Yountville, CA 94599 – www.tomscottvineyard.com – (707) 944–1850 – Hours: Appointment – This is a small family vineyard that makes one Cabernet blend, tasted with the owners. When you visit plan to buy.

Trefethen Vineyards – Historic Winery – Wines: Dry Riesling, Viognier, Chardonnay, Pinot Noir, Cabernet Franc, Merlot, Cabernet Sauvignon, Late Harvest Riesling – 1160 Oak Knoll Ave. Napa CA 94558 – www.trefethen.com – (707) 255–7700 Hours: 10:00am – 4:30pm Appointment – They are in an historic restored, gravity fed winery from the 1800's. The first floor is the barrel room that you see through a glass wall. The tasting room upstairs is spacious, and they make estate wines of high quality, inlcuding an outstanding Riesling, rare in Napa. Navigation Tip: As you come north on Highway 29, you turn right at the light at Oak Knoll Ave. The entrance is on the left.

Tres Perlas – Los Carneros Small Family for Collectors – Wines: Bordeaux and Burgundy Blends – 625 Imperial Way #6, Napa, CA 94559 – www.tresperlas.com – (707) 255-0786

Tres Sabores – Small Rustic Charm – Wines: Zinfandel, Cabernet Sauvignon, Petite Syrah, Petite Verdot, Sauvignon Blanc 1620 South Whitehall Lane Saint Helena CA 94574 – www.tressabores.com – (707) 967–8027 – Hours: by Appointment This is a charming family winery on prime bench land with old Zin and Cab vines. In nice weather, the tasting is done outside at a picnic table, under huge olive trees. In cool weather, the tasting is done in the winery. The hillsides are planted with grapes and pomegranates. Watch for the sheep in the vineyards as you arrive because this is a working ranch. This is hands–on winemaking so if you can, visit here during crush.

Trinchero Napa Valley – Saint Helena Wine and Food – Wines: Cabernet Sauvignon, Meritage, Sauvignon Blanc, Merlot, Petite Verdot – 3070 St Helena Highway (Highway 29). Saint Helena CA 94574 – www.trincherowinery.com – (707) 963–3104 – This hospitality center just north of Saint Helena, showcases their best wines & culinary center.

Trinitas Cellars – At the Meritage Resort – Wines: Chardonnay, Pinot Noir, Mataro, Petit Syrah, Zinfandel, Blends – 875 Bordeaux Way Napa CA 94558 www.trinitascellars.com – (707) 251 –1956 – Hours: 12:00pm – 8:00pm. Their tasting room is in a cave behind the hotel that they share with the spa. So many of the people who stay at the resort visit them. They produce less common varietals and they are worth the visit just for that, although the entire experience is cool.

Truchard Vineyard – Carneros Gem – Wines: Chardonnay, Roussanne, Pinot Noir, Syrah, Zinfandel, Merlot, Cabernet Franc, Cabernet Sauvignon, Petit Verdot, Tempranillo, Olive Oil – 3234 Old Sonoma Road Napa CA 94559 – www.truchardvineyards.com – (707) 253–7153 – Hours: Appointment – The Truchard family makes wonderful wines, complex, delicious and interesting, at their property in the hills of Los Carneros. They have owned the land since 1974 and started making their own wines in 1989. They make a Cabernet Sauvignon, which is rare in Carneros, an area generally too cool for this heat loving grape. The tasting room is basic, the caves are nice, and in good weather they taste outside on the lawn beside the house.

Tulocay Winery – Eastern Napa – Wines: Pinot Noir, Cabernet Sauvignon, Merlot, Syrah, Zinfandel, Chardonnay – 1426 Coombsville Rd Napa CA 94558 – www.tulocaywinery.com – (707) 255-4064 – Hours: Appointment – This is old school Napa, totally authentic and close to the downtown.

Turnbull Wine Cellars – Photo Gallery in the Middle of Oakville Wines: Sauvignon Blanc, Old Bull Red, Viognier, Toroso, Cabernet Sauvignon, Merlot, Barbera, Syrah – 8210 St Helena Highway (Highway 29). Oakville CA 94562 – www.turnbullwines.com – (707) 963–5839 – Hours: 10:00am to 4:30pm – The original owner, William Turnbull, was the architect who designed numerous wineries including the Cakebread winery next door, so note the similarity. It features a photography gallery'. They have a nice tasting room and grounds.

Twenty Rows / Vinoce – Tannery Row Commercial Space Tasting Room – Wines: Bordeaux and Burgundy Blends – 68 South Coombs Street, L6 Napa, CA 94559 – www.twentyrows.com – (707)–265–7750 – Hours: 11:00am to 6:00pm Wednesday – Saturday, 12:00pm to 6:00pm Sunday Appointment.

Twomey Cellars – Merlot Focus – Wines: Merlot, Pinot Noir, Sauvignon Blanc – 1183 Dunaweal Lane Calistoga CA 94515 – www.twomeycellars.com – (707) 942-2489 – Hours: 9:00am – 4:00pm This winery is associated with Silver Oak. They created this winery to specialize in Merlot based wines. The Twomey winery in northern Sonoma specializes in Pinot Noir.

Varozza Vineyards – Saint Helena Dry Farmed Five Generations – Wines: Bordeaux and Burgundy – 514 Pratt Ave, St Helena, CA 94574 – www.varozzavineyards.com – (707) 963-0331 – A family estate winery north of downtown Saint Helena. They are traditional Italian American growers who started here in the late 1800's. Dry farming produces less grapes that are known for their rich flavors. The wines are moderately priced.

Velo Vino (Clif Family) – Downtown Saint Helena Tasting Room and Retail Shop – Wines: Cabernet Sauvignon – 709 Main St, St Helena, CA 94574 –www.cliffamily.com – (707) 968-0625 – Hours: 10:00am to 5:00pm – Bike Rental Packages, Breakfast Pairings and Cheese and Jam Boards – This is the family that makes the Clif Bar, which you will find for sale there.

Venge Vineyards – Wines: Bordeaux and Burgundy –4708 Silverado Trail N, Calistoga, CA 94515 – www.vengevineyards.com (707) 942-9100 – Hours: 10:00am – 4:30pm Appointment – The Venges, father and son, are well known consulting winemakers. This is the son's winery situated in a modern metal building in the northern part of the valley. Fortunately, the tastings take place in a cozy house next door.

Vermeil Wines – Downtown Napa Tasting Room – Wines: Sauvignon Blanc, Charbono, Cabernet Franc, Cabernet Sauvignon, Zinfandel – 1018 First Street, Napa, CA 94559 – www.vermeilwines.com – (707) 254-9881 – Hours: 11:00am – 11:00pm Appointment – Owned by former football coach Dick Vermeil.

VGS Potelle – Saint Helena Tasting Room – Wines: Bordeaux and Burgundy – 1200 Dowdell Lane, Saint Helena CA 94574 www.vgschateaupotelle.com – (707) 255-9440 – Hours: 10:00am – 5:00pm Appointment – Marvelous wines with a French style by a French wine maker who has making wine here for many years. The initials stand for 'Very Good Shit!'

Viader – Deer Park Cab Franc – Wines: Bordeaux, Syrah, Tempranillo – 1120 Deer Park Road Deer Park CA 94574 – www.viader.com – (707) 963-3816 – Hours: 10:00am–4:30pm Appointment – This family-run winery makes Cabernet Franc blends. Great views! The gate is on the left at a sharp, climbing curve so be careful of the cars coming down the hill. Their neighboring winery was destroyed in the 2020 Glass fire.

Vice Versa Winery – Collectors – Saint Helena Town Tasting Room – Wines: Bordeaux Blends – 707-968-5620 – Hours: Appointment www.viceversawine.com – They have vineyards in Calistoga and produce marvelous wines.

Villa Ragazzi – Very Small Oakville Winery – Wines: Sangiovese – 7878 Money Rd, Napa, CA 94558 – www.villaragazziwine.com – (707) 486-3184 – Hours: Appointment – The name means 'house of the kids', this is a tiny family estate vineyard owned by the winemakers, where they make just over a hundred cases of wine yearly.

Vin Roc Wine Caves – Collectors in Southeast Napa Valley Wines: Bordeaux – 4069 Atlas Peak Rd, Napa, CA 94558 – www.vinrocnapa.com – (707) 265-0943 – Appt.

Vincent Arroyo Winery – Calistoga – Wines: Cabernet Sauvignon, Merlot, Petite Syrah, Chardonnay, Sangiovese, Port, Blends 2361 Greenwood Ave. Calistoga CA 94515 – www.vincentarroyo.com (707) 942-6995 – Hours: 10:00am – 4:00pm Appointment – They are located just north of downtown Calistoga south of Chateau Montelena. The overall feeling is that of a small working winery without any pretensions. They are in the second generation now.

Vine Cliff Winery – A Yountville Jewel – Wines: Cabernet Sauvignon, Chardonnay, Merlot. – 7400 Silverado Trail Yountville CA 94599 – www.vinecliff.com – (707) 944-1364 – Hours: 10:00am – 5:00pm Appointment – This is a jewel of a winery in its own canyon just off the Silverado Trail, north of the Yountville Cross Road They have beautiful gardens and gorgeous caves that are part of the tour. Their gate is normally closed so call ahead. They have not focused on estate tastings since they opened a tasting room across from V. Sattui, but they still do them there.

Vine Hill Ranch – Collectors Oakville – Wines: Cabernet Sauvignon – www.vinehillranch.com – 707-944-8130 – The family has owned these vineyards since the 1950's, and they supply grapes to many local wineries.

Vineyard 29 – Look for the Sign because they are located at 2929 Highway 29 – Wines: Cabernet Sauvignon, Cabernet Franc, Sauvignon Blanc, Zinfandel, Blends – 2929 Highway 29 North Saint Helena CA 94574 – www.vineyard29.com – (707) 963-9292 – Hours: Tuesday–Saturday Appointment – This state of the art winery north of downtown Saint Helena is on a hillside with great views of the valley. Plan for a tour of the caves where the tasting takes place.

Vineyard 7 and 8 – Collectors – Spring Mountain Collectors Wines: Bordeaux – Spring Mountain Road, Saint Helena CA 94574 – www.vineyard7and8.com – (707) 963-9425 – Hours: Appointment, closed weekends – This winery at the top of Spring Mountain is for the enthusiast. From the front it looks like a house, but from the back it is obviously a serious winery with great views. The name comes from the Asian numerological significance of those two numbers.

Vineyardist – Collectors – www.thevineyardist.com – (707) 942-0120 – Hours: 10:00am – 2:00pm Appt – The original vineyards were planted in the 1880's by a Danish ship captain off Petrified Forest Road in Calistoga.

Vintner's Collective Tasting Room – Numerous premium labels in a wonderful old building in downtown Napa – 1245 Main Street Napa CA 94559 – www.vintnerscollective.com – (707) 255-7150 – Hours: 11:00am to 6:00pm. One of Napa's oldest collective tasting rooms.

V. Madrone – Small with Lots of History – Wines: Chardonnay, Cabernet Sauvignon, Petite Syrah, Zinfandel. – 3199 Saint Helena Highway North Saint Helena CA 94574 – www.vmadrone.com – (877) 994-6311 – Hours: Appointment – This is a small, charming premium winery, although the vineyards are nearby, just north of downtown St. Helena. AXR winery is located on the same property.

Volker Eisele – Collectors – Wines: Bordeaux, Burgundy – Lower Chiles Valley Road, Saint Helena CA 94574 – www.volkereiselefamilyestate.com – (707) 965-9485 – – This is a small, premium winery in the hills of eastern Napa. Their redwood winery barn was constructed in the 1800's. Allow time for the drive. *Note: 2020 Glass fire came through there.*

V. Sattui Winery – The Famous Deli and Winery – Wines: The valley's widest selection – 1111 White Lane Saint Helena 94574 (On Highway 29) – www.vsattui.com – (707) 963–7774 – Hours: 9:00am – 6:00pm, 9:00am – 5:00pm in Winter – This may be Napa's busiest winery thanks to its large deli and picnic tables. Centrally located, the wines are also middle of the road, and very drinkable with a reserve tasting room by appointment. The property is pretty, although it suffers from the crowds. The founder owns Castello di Amorosa in Calistoga. They are in a commercial zone, and not in the Agricultural Preserve. The other property with that 'deli' exemption is Brasswood.

Wheeler Farms – Saint Helena Collectors – Wines: Bordeaux and Burgundy – 588 Zinfandel Lane, Saint Helena CA 94574 www.wheelerfarmswine.com – (707) 200–8500 – Hours: 10:00am – 4:00pm Appointment – This newer winery from a long-time wine making family is a biodynamic gem. It is very convenient south of St. Helana and the property is extensively planted with food plants. The Winery is state of the art.

Whetstone – Tasting Site in an Historic Building with Burgundy Style wines – Wines: Pinot Noir, Chardonnay – 1075 Atlas Peak Road, Napa CA 94558 – www.whetstonewinecellars.com - (707) 254–0600 Hours: 10:30am – 3:30pm Appointment – Tastings generally take place outside in their garden in front of the old distillery building from the late 1800's. It is in the south eastern corner of the valley just north of Monticello Road, which is the eastern extension of Trancas Avenue, which is the northern edge of the City of Napa. The vineyards and winery are at a different location. Mapa D

Whitehall Lane Winery – Fun with Wonderful Wines – Wines: Cabernet Sauvignon, Merlot, Chardonnay, Belmuscato Dessert Wine – 1563 St Helena Highway (Highway 29). South Saint Helena CA 94574 – www.whitehalllane.com – (707) 963–7035 Hours: 11:00am – 5:45pm – The modern tasting room has a bit of a bar feel, but it allows diverse groups to mix.

White Rock Vineyards – Soda Canyon – Wines: Bordeaux and Burgundy – 1112 Loma Vista Dr Napa, CA 94558 – www.whiterockvineyards.com – (707) 257–7922 – Hours: 10:00am – 5:00pm Appointment – A small family winery in the hills in southeastern Napa off Soda Canyon Road.

William Cole – Saint Helena Collectors – Cabernet Blends – 2849 St Helena Hwy, St Helena, CA 94574 – www.williamcolevineyards.com – (707) 963-6100 – These fifth generation Napa winemakers produce less than a thousand cases of wine from three small vineyards around the county. The building was constructed in 1873 and the upper part is a home, while the ground floor is the winery. William and Cole are the first names of the father and son team who make the wine. They have a beautifully appointed tasting room. The winery is wonderfully convenient, located on the west side of Highway 29 north of Saint Helena, by the intersection of Deer Park Road. They share the driveway with the stone Morlet Winery, built in 1880, which is more visible from the road.

William Harrison Vineyards – A Great Story – Wines: Cabernet Sauvignon, Cabernet Franc, Chardonnay – 1443 Silverado Trail Saint Helena CA 94574 – www.whwines.com – (707) 963–8310 – Hours: 11–5 Thursday – Monday – This is a rustic and slightly eccentric tasting room for a family with a great story that goes back to the 1500's in Italy. The wines are interesting, and the location is great. Watch out for the stuffed bear that comes with a story! They have a nice patio for tastings and it is surrounded by their Cabernet Franc vineyards.

William Hill Estate – Southern Valley – Wines: Chardonnay, Merlot, Cabernet Sauvignon, Cabernet Franc, Malbec, Petit Verdot, Estate Meritage – 1761 Atlas Peak Road Napa CA 94558 www.williamhillestate.com – (707) 265–3024 – Hours: 10:00am–5:00pm Appointment. This is a great site, with a picnic area under an arbor. It is owned by Gallo.

The Wine Thief – Downtown Tasting Room at the Oxbow – Wines: Cabernet Sauvignon, Burgundy – 708 1st St, Napa, CA 94559 (707) 666–2650 – Hours: 10:00am – 6:00pm Appt.

Yates Family Vineyard – Mt Veeder – Wines: Cabernet Sauvignon, Cabernet Franc, Merlot – 3104 Redwood Rd Napa – www.YatesFamilyVineyard.com – (707) 226–1800 – Hours: Appointment – A small family winery in southwestern Napa, on the way to Mount Veeder.

Y. Rousseau – Corporate Park – Wines: Bordeaux, General French – 902 Enterprise Way Suite O Napa, CA 94558 – www.yrousseauwines.com – (707) 332–4524 – Hours: 9:00am – 4:00pm Monday–Saturday Appointment.

Young Inglewood – Collectors – Wines: Bordeaux and Burgundy – 1919 Inglewood Ave, Saint Helena CA 94574 – www.younginglewood.com – (707) 200-4572 – A premium winery selling through allocation.

Zakin Family Estate – By Allocation – Wines: Cabernet Sauvignon – 290 Crystal Springs Rd Saint Helena CA 94574 – www.zakinwines.com – (415)-793-6354 – An ultra-premium family winery using the winemaker Phillipe Melka.

ZD Wines – Silverado Savvy – Wines: Chardonnay, Pinot Noir, Cabernet Sauvignon – 8383 Silverado Trail Napa CA 94558 www.zdwines.com – (800) 487-7757 – Hours: 10:00am –4:30pm Appointment – They have a friendly, relaxed, stylish tasting room, with a patio on the second story that overlooks their organic vineyards, a nice staff, and some good wine. They often get missed because they are below the road on a downhill section of the Silverado Trail, so you do not see them until you are at the driveway. They are to the south of Mumm Napa on the Silverado Trail. the name comes from the term 'Zero Defects', because the founders came from the aeronautic industry. The wine maker is from their third generation. This is a winery worth visiting, organic, with a great family history. As you leave notice the sign 'Organic since 1999'.

AmicisTours.com

A Tour Guide's Napa Valley
A Tour Guide's Sonoma Wine Country
Sonoma Navigator, Maps & Highlights
Napa Navigator, Maps & Highlights
Wine Country in Shorts, A Tour Guide's Stories

Watch the Author's TV Show 'Wine, Wine & Water'

PlanetaryCalendar.com
Published Annually since 1949

Planetary Calendar Astrology Forecasts & Health Hints
Two Wall Sizes, a Pocket Size, a Day Planner &
a Digital Version for your Phone and Computer
The Companion Book
'Planetary Calendar Astrology,
Moving Beyond Observation to Action'

Watch the Author's Weekly Forecasts & Astro Portraits
at Planetary Calendar Astrology

SpaceAndTime.com

From the 'Tango' Series
Feng Shui and the Tango, The Dance of Design
Feng Shui and the Tango, The Essential Chapters
25th Anniversary Edition
FS&T Prosperity Lessons
FS&T Happiness Lessons
The Dream Desk Quiz
Creating Clarity

About the Authors

Ralph and Lahni DeAmicis backed into writing tour and travel books by starting to create a book about winery buildings for their series on Feng Shui, but the research was going excruciatingly slow. While the winery staff knew the wines, they rarely knew about the buildings. Then one day, while coming out of the Stag's Leap Wine Cellars, Ralph chatted up a local limousine driver who was a wealth of information about interesting winery buildings, apparently that knowledge was part of a tour guide's toolbox.

Seeing a research opportunity that would also put some money in their pockets, Ralph got a part time job driving tours, coming home daily with notes and photographs of the wineries. As he navigated his way around the various valleys, they realized that even though the wineries are the biggest attraction, there wasn't a good 'winery' tour book. So, their project about buildings morphed into their first guide book in 2008, becoming the first in a series of updates and improvements.

After two years of touring for other companies Ralph & Lahni decided to start their own tour company, Amicis Tours, to make the continuing research easier. They soon realized that it's a fun business that brings them to beautiful places while connecting them to the winemaking community. In 2012 they started producing the TV show 'Wine Country at Work' which allowed them to more deeply explore topics that they found interesting.

Find their books and videos at:
www.AmicisTours.com
**Cuore Libre Publishing
Books and Calendars**

www.ingramcontent.com/pod-product-compliance
Lightning Source LLC
Chambersburg PA
CBHW051600010526
44118CB00023B/2767